The Image of Europe in Henry James

The
Image of Europe
in
HENRY JAMES

CHRISTOF WEGELIN

1958
SOUTHERN METHODIST UNIVERSITY PRESS
DALLAS

Library of Congress Catalog Card Number: 58-9271

To Caroline

Acknowledgments

I AM GRATEFUL to The Johns Hopkins University and to Princeton
University for grants which gave me the freedom needed to begin
this book, and to the Graduate School of the University of Oregon
for grants which helped me to finish it; to the editors of *ELH,
Symposium, Nineteenth-Century Fiction,* the *Northwest Review,*
and the *Jahrbuch für Amerikastudien* for permission to use materials which have appeared in their pages; to the staffs of the Library
of The Johns Hopkins University, the Library of the Peabody
Institute, the Enoch Pratt Free Library, the Princeton University
Library, the Stanford University Library, the Library of Congress,
and the Library of the University of Oregon for many courtesies;
to Jacqueline Naggiar Van Voris for clerical and bibliographical
help; to Martha Schmitt for expert skill in making the Index; to
Margaret L. Hartley for editorial wisdom; and to my wife, Caroline
Wegelin, for proofreading matters familiar to her.

To name all those — including my teachers and students—
who have stimulated and enlightened me is not possible, though in
the Notes I have tried to acknowledge my debts to what others

have written. But I am happy to have this opportunity of expressing my gratitude to the following: Charles Anderson, Richard Blackmur, Ernest Dilworth, Roy Pearce, Willard Thorp, and the late Raymond Dexter Havens—all of whom, to my profit, read the manuscript in an earlier form.

C. W.

Contents

The Image of Europe in Henry James

Prologue

"ONE OF the responsibilities" of being an American, James wrote in the early 1870's, "is fighting against a superstitious valuation of Europe."[1] The statement was not only a prophecy of his own career; it was a comment also on the writers who preceded him. For the acceptance of some such responsibility toward Europe was not simply the prejudice of an "expatriate." Many American writers of the nineteenth century felt the need to define their own and their country's relation to Europe, and few thought that it was their duty as Americans to turn their backs on her. The fact needs to be constantly remembered if James's relation to America and Europe is to be understood. For although his case was special, it was an American case.

The "responsibility" James spoke of followed inevitably from the fact that American culture was transplanted. "Cosmopolitanism" has from colonial days to our own been an issue in American life. "Our people," Emerson said, "have their intellectual culture from one country and their duties from another." This is why from the beginning our colleges, for instance, have fostered an awareness of our cultural ties with the "old world" and with England in particular, why the booksellers of the early Republic could complain of "the rage of the American people for foreign productions,"[2] and why in the twentieth century some American authors still have to make a name in England (Frost) or in France (Faulkner) before their countrymen take them seriously. Add to the colonial origins of American civilization the material preoccupations natural to a pioneering people, and no more is needed to explain why American intellectuals should have persisted for so long in hankering for the cultural fleshpots of Europe, or why even Whitman could say that "the best of America is the best cosmopolitanism."[3]

Once "cosmopolitanism" is recognized as part of the national tradition, it ceases to serve as a measure of divergence from sound "Americanism." While the impulses of the Revolution were still vivid, politics furnished a solid sense of national identity. But later, when George III had paled into a schoolbook symbol, when England became more democratic while in America a new industrial plutocracy tarnished the early agrarian republicanism, the sense of kinship with England reasserted itself despite recurrent animosities. Holmes furnishes an example of how far this sense could go: "As the New England characteristics are gradually superseded by those of other races, other forms of belief, and other associations," he wrote in 1886, "the time may come when a New Englander will feel more as if he were among his own people in London than in one of our seaboard cities." The "ties of blood," the "common religious and political traditions," he felt, would continue to draw Americans of English stock back to the "old home" of their fathers, "delightful in itself" and "infinitely desirable" because so close to "all that is most interesting in Europe." Repeated ocean crossings were inconvenient and dangerous; the causes which had driven the original settlers from their "dearly loved native land" had ceased to operate since religious freedom was now "found in England as fully as in America"; and it followed, thus Holmes cheerfully predicted, that a stream of permanent "re-migrants" to ancestral England was almost bound to balance before long the stream of alien immigrants to the United States.[4] Curious in their reaches and betraying a vision of history somewhat incomplete, such views of an aging Brahmin might provoke trans-Mississippian laughter. But in the East, the admiration of what Emerson had called the "best of actual nations" was widespread. And even Mark Twain succumbed: "I would a good deal rather live here," he wrote in 1872 from London.[5]

The middle classes, moreover, had their own Anglophile tradition. In 1857—to cite a striking example—George Francis Train, who described himself as the graduate of a Boston "counting house," gave in a volume of travel letters a "merchant's" version of the Anglo-Saxon "community of feeling." The common cultural tradition evidently had little personal meaning for Train; so much is revealed by the tone of his facile references to England's "grand old castles, her classic lakes where poets most do congregate." Nor was "the community of feeling" political. For although from Austria to France the good American had vaguely been aware of "cities full of pictures and sculpture, with history written in blood" until in Dover he finally sniffed "free air" again, his admiration for England was not based on love of liberty. Rather it was a mercantile appreciation of England's imperialist achievement. Nothing makes this clearer than the interpretation of the American Revolution which Train supplies in his preface: "The revolution was merely an animated conversation" between "partners" who introduced "shot and cannon" to "give emphasis to the debate"; and "when the disputed 'point' was settled, old England rose with renewed vigor, in Young America"—the junior partner "who manages the western branch of the old concern." As Train is writing, the diplomatic relations between the two countries are strained again, the partnership is threatened with "self-destruction," and Americans are therefore admonished to remember their "proud old mother" and to

"... join the Stars and Stripes and Cross in one fraternal band,
'Till Anglo-Saxon faith and laws illumine every land."[6]

The conflict between an American's "duties" and his "intellectual culture" which Emerson had spoken of, between the native and the European components of the American tradition, is here resolved into the breezy air of Anglo-Saxon imperialism. The intellectual tradition itself has evaporated; neither poetry nor political principle is left, not even history, except of conquest and trade. But while Train is worlds apart from men of letters like Holmes or Lowell or James, he nevertheless suggests that in order to think of England and, less immediately, of Europe as the cradle of his own civilization, an American did not have to be an aesthete unable to accommodate himself to the realities of his country.

Yet, for the artist and intellectual the problem had a particular urgency. Holmes again furnishes the type. After returning from Europe in the summer of 1886, he complained that "the New World keeps the imagination on a plain and scanty diet, compared to the rich traditional and historic food which furnishes the banquets of the Old World." Cooper in *Notions of the Americans* and Hawthorne in the preface to *The Marble Faun* had made similar complaints, and James's diagnosis of the difficulty posed for the American novelist by the "simple, democratic, thinly-composed society" of his country has achieved notoriety.[7] But after seven years abroad, Hawthorne, too, had come home rather unwillingly. "I wonder that we Americans love our country at all," he had written in his notebook. And attributing American patriotism to "the singularity of our form of government," he had concluded that "if other nations had similar institutions—if England, especially, were a Democracy—we should as readily make ourselves at home in another country as now in a new state." Similarly Charles Eliot Norton was to confess that he felt "American only so far as our political and social systems are."[8]

We may like it or not. We may share Stanley T. Williams' belief that in a sense the "cosmopolitans" of the nineteenth century "were the true founders of our modern literary culture." Or we may feel with R. P. Blackmur that the expatriates' belief that culture "could be *brought from* abroad" was a delusion—if indeed the two views are conflicting.[9] Europe, at any rate, was culturally an American concern and problem. And with the strengthening of national identity the problem became if anything more, not less, acute. This is why James in 1903 could wonder at the "large, quiet, pleasant, easy solution" at which Longfellow had arrived. Had Longfellow "worked up his American consciousness to that mystic point" at which "it could feel nothing but continuity and congruity with his European?" James had to confess that he did not know. If the delightful "ambiguity" of Longfellow's "liberal existence" seemed "a piece of the old world smoothly fitted into the new, so it might quite as well have been a piece of the new fitted just as intimately, into the old." But if Longfellow's case defied analysis, plenty of other cases did not. The "social, personal, aesthetic" relation of "the American world to the European" made "as charming a subject as the student of manners, morals, personal adventures, the history of taste, the development of a society, need wish to take up."[10] James said it feelingly. He had made and was still making the American in Europe one of the major subjects of his fiction. The "great lighted and decorated scene" of Europe, as he said elsewhere, served as an "effective *repoussoir*" for the American character,[11] and the American character was one of James's ruling interests. Another was the nature of morality, its relation to manners and to civilization. And the dramatic analysis of the "international situation" in the end served him indeed primarily as a means of coming to grips with those two vital subjects. Besides, it was one's responsibility to fight against a "superstitious valuation" of the old world.

To trace this fight in James is my purpose in the following chapters—to trace James's relation to traditional American attitudes toward Europe and the development of his treatment of the "international situation" from more or less conventional beginnings to the conceptual and formal complexity of his latest fiction. The American desire to come to terms with the problem of Europe had given rise to certain images of Europe, all dominated by the consciousness of a lingering past. In his earliest international fiction James reflects some of these images. But what distinguishes his treatment of Europe from that of earlier Americans is the progressive deepening of his vision. His unusual opportunities of observation enabled him to recognize the element of "superstition" in the earlier American images of Europe, their subjective elements as typical of the American imagination. Soon, therefore, he made them part of the subject matter of his fiction. At the same time his preoccupation with the American character asserted itself, and his major protagonist in the international drama became the young American girl. At the height of his career, after the interruption of his dramatic years and of his concern with purely English subjects, he once more returned to international contrasts, though now they served him primarily as a means to the larger end of analyzing the nature of morality. The last three novels of his maturity are of course far removed from his early comedies of the international. But some of the old American images of Europe reappear in them, though greatly transformed by their function in James's design. And the relation of these novels to the canon of his international fiction clarifies the essential unity of their conception.

"When vigorous writers have reached maturity," James wrote in his first essay on Turgenieff in the 1870's, "we are at liberty to look in their works for some expression of a total view of the world they have been so actively observing."[12] His own treatment of the meeting of America and Europe allows us to gather something like a total view of his relation to the two worlds once separated by the Atlantic. The first thing it reveals is the expatriate's strong commitment to American modes of thinking and feeling. The second, a final shift in the focus of his contrasting evaluation of America and Europe, may suggest what values so attracted him to the Old World that he continued to make his life there.

I   *"Superstitious Valuations"*

SHORTLY AFTER the Revolution a strain of nostalgia crept into American writings about England. The conflict with England had forced Americans to cease thinking of themselves as "sharing the rich inheritance of English history" and "contributing to its enlargement and perpetuation";[1] and soon such writers as Paulding, Tyler, and later Cooper were busy defending the newly independent Republic against English and other European critics. But after the War of 1812, the revolutionary desire for liberation could give way to the desire of a politically independent society for Old World culture, and the interest in England was not long in spreading to the Continent.

This shift is illustrated in Irving's turn from native American matters in the *Salmagundi* papers (1807-8) and the Knickerbocker *History of New York* (1809) to English and European scenes in *The Sketch Book* (1819-20) and the later writings. For Irving's first trip to Europe evidently does not explain the change in his interests. His whirlwind tour of Italy in 1804 and the weeks in Paris following it had led to nothing. But in *The Sketch Book* he struck a note that was to reverberate well into the later decades of the century. The contemporary American magazines, notoriously biased as they were by political, sectional, and personal considerations, might disagree about his merits as a reporter of English life; but by 1850 *The Sketch Book* had achieved sixteen American editions, *Bracebridge Hall* (1822) eleven, *Tales of a Traveller* (1824) at least ten. Evidently, the food Irving dished up pleased American stomachs.

What kind of food was it that Americans found so palatable? Hazlitt, in a remark which other Englishmen were to echo in connection with other American pictures of England, put the recipe in a nutshell. Irving's writings, he said in 1825, "are literally *anachronisms.*" "Instead of looking round to see what *we are,* he sets to work to describe us as *we were*—at second hand."[2] Hazlitt was right, for although Irving delighted in new scenes and could write of them with great charm, his description of himself as a born sight-seer does not touch the center of his inspiration. What chiefly interested him in Europe, he said in *Bracebridge Hall,* were the "peculiarities which distinguish an old country and an old state of society from a new one" because "to a man from a new country all old things are in a manner new." But what in effect was new to the American traveler in Europe were the visibly lingering traces of a past he knew from books. Irving's descriptions of England were "second hand" quite simply because his inspiration came ultimately all from his childhood reading.

Nothing makes this clearer than the contrast between the personal warmth with which he wrote of England and Spain and the flat conventionality with which he treated the rest of Europe. He had seen Italy and France and Germany, too; yet between 80 and 90 per cent of his European sketches and stories deal with England and Spain. Above all, his gothic tales of "Italian Banditti" betray no interest in the Italian character; his comments on the French are limited to a few commonplaces about their gaiety and, of course, their incorrigible urbanity in matters of love—this last sounding the note of what James was to call the "dreadful little old tradition" of Paris as the "consecrated scene of rash infatuations."[3] As for Germany, despite the temporary interest in German legends and romance which his *Journals* reveal, despite the fact that many of his short stories go back to German sources, in the writings published during his lifetime Irving left no picture of the country and the people. It was only when, in 1826, his wanderings brought him to Spain that his imagination took fire again. Only in *The Alhambra* (1832) do we again meet the joyful recognition of the familiar in the strange which animates the best of his English pieces.

The reason is simple: Irving's childhood reading had in the main been limited to the British classics and the chivalric chronicles of Spain; and in those two countries, therefore, he felt that history and poetry had spread their "charm over every-day life."[4] This is why about England and Spain he could write in the language which was to become the stock in trade of many an American traveler— of "the charms of storied and poetical association" and of the "mementos of the past." This is why whatever serious concern with national character his writings do show is again limited to England and Spain. For what he sought in Europe were the scenes of the events he had read about as a boy—"the very place" once haunted by Don Juan[5] or the very forest once ringing to the cries of Robin Hood. Now and then the scenes themselves could at first glance be disappointing: the northern border country of England, for instance, was "a mere succession of gray waving hills" and the "far-famed Tweed" a mere "naked stream" between "bare hills"— until he remembered the associations and all became more charming to him "than the richest scenery."[6] Then indeed, when his imagination was thus moved, he observed vividly. Then he gave his readers a sense of observed reality. Then, despite occasional objections to his flunky interest in the English gentry, American reviewers would praise the "accuracy and fidelity" of his observations.[7]

Irving created a fashion. But while his pictures of England and Spain were animated by the imagination, while he was able to fuse the inner and the outer vision, writers less passionately antiquarian were likely to vulgarize the manner and to turn the Europe of poetic and historical memories into a mere museum of moss-grown walls and crumbling ruins. Sometimes the references to the "associations" remained indeed little more than a polite obeisance to convention administered before going on to more genuine interests.[8] Nevertheless, awkwardly or unwillingly, American travelers writing about Europe again and again administered the bow, as if they could not help themselves.[9] Unless indeed, like Longfellow, they consciously sought to capitalize on the fashion. Longfellow had planned his *Outre Mer* (1833-34) as "a kind of Sketch-Book of France, Spain, and Italy."[10] Imitating his model even to its outward makeup, he too reveled in the famous "mementos" of the past and pictured himself as a pilgrim to all the things he had "read of, but had not seen."[11] But *Outre Mer* lacks the spontaneity and charm of *The Sketch Book*. For Longfellow had little of Irving's single vision: he was more bookish than the older author and at the same time more aware of contemporary conditions in Europe.

His private journals and his letters could indeed contain the kind of intelligence Mark Twain was later to exploit. From Florence, for instance, he had written to his mother: "Can you believe that the Arno—'that glassy river'" is a "stream of yellow, muddy water almost entirely dry in summer" and that "all the rigmarole of midnight song and soft serenade" is "not altogether so delightful in reality as we sometimes fancy?" But in 1828 the time was not yet ripe for such disclosures. Longfellow ended his letter significantly: "I must not tell tales! I may spoil the market for some beautiful effusion." And when he came to piece together a version of his "Pilgrimage Beyond the Sea" for public consumption, he expurgated his record—and spoke of "Florence the Fair," with its "magnificent Duomo," its art treasures, "its delightful environs," its "pure air," but of the muddy Arno and other disappointing realities not a word.[12]

If Longfellow observed more soberly than Irving had done, he subordinated the results to the "glorious world of poetry, romance, and dreams."[13] The fashion seems to have persisted throughout the century. For although it was challenged now and then and sooner or later *Innocents Abroad* was bound to be written, even Mark Twain was quite capable of being impressed by a "picturesque ruin," a "venerable arch," by "visions of fabled fairyland," or—since even he employed the standard formula—by the sight of "something which you have *read* about somewhere but never seen."[14] And if he lampooned the hackneyed profession of an attitude emptied of genuine feeling, he had his forerunners. As early as 1830 John Neal, protesting that he did not see "a fortieth part" of what *The Sketch Book* had led him to expect, had poked fun at the pilgrims who, "lips blue and teeth chattering—perhaps with awe —perhaps with cold," admired the "toy-shop" show of Westminster Abbey.[15] But few writers came so close to Mark Twain's tone. Rather, as the century progressed, a new type of travel book appeared, written by and for middle-class Americans, and intended to present things as they were, without romantic frills.[16]

From the start, moreover, the image of Europe as the locus of America's cultural past had been balanced by a counterimage of the social dead hand of the past, the sense of kinship with England and Europe by a national pride founded on political grounds.[17] The two strains could exist side by side without serious tension. But the growth of social democracy under Jackson led to a nostalgia different from Irving's—not for the scenes and monuments rich in poetic and historical associations, but for the social distinctions and amenities of high European society. And when the republican pride in America's political departure was joined to the admiration of aristocratic manners, the emotional tensions and conflicting loyalties of a fundamental American problem arose. Like the Irvingesque nostalgia, they were to serve James as the stuff of comedy. The significance of manners in the scheme of civilization was indeed to concern him more and more as time went on. And

the difference between his approaches to the problem and its manifestation in such early figures as Willis and Cooper measures in a
way the growth of national maturity.

During the 1830's N. P. Willis' chatty travel letters, later collected under the title of *Pencillings by the Way,* entertained the
readers of the New York *Mirror* for almost five years. On first
coming to Europe, he had rhapsodized in the expected fashion about
"the presence of all that we have seen in pictures and read of in
books, but consider as the representations and descriptions of ages
gone by." In Italy he had made pilgrimages to the tombs of Petrarch
and Juliet and to the spots made famous by Childe Harold. But
gradually his interest in social matters asserted itself, and although
the first distant sight of St. Paul's and Westminster delighted him
by its storied familiarity, his reports from England speak mostly of
life in high society. Their popularity justified his belief that it was
the "society that most interests Americans."

But Willis' fiction on European themes gives the lie to the
charmed tone of his *Pencillings.* In story after story the heartless
snobbery of fashionable European society is his theme: again and
again one of "nature's noblemen" proves his superiority over the
"artificial" social distinctions of Europe. And in *Paul Fane,* a later
novel, the protest against institutionalized "social position" is even
more bitter.[18] The two reactions to European "high-life," the admiration of its elegancies and the repugnance against the caste system,
inextricably entangled as they are in Willis, seem to have been
spontaneous emotional responses to different aspects of the same
thing. In Cooper's social fiction, on the other hand, two similar
strains are parts of a carefully formulated, if not wholly consistent, theory.

When Cooper took his family to Europe in 1826, his purpose
was simply to improve his own health, to educate his children in
the languages, and to secure English publishing rights. But soon his
patriotism was challenged by European hostility toward America.
Hence, in 1828, his *Notions of the Americans,* a volume of essays

in defense of America. From this point on, social and political criticism of Europe crept into his fiction too, until in *The Bravo* (1831), *The Heidenmauer* (1832), and *The Headsman* (1833) he actually turned to European subjects. He had come to feel that America's political achievement was endangered by a "slavish dependence on foreign opinion." And intent on counteracting this danger, he designed his three European novels as a series "in which American opinion should be brought to bear on European facts" so as to illustrate the evils of "hereditary rank."[19]

After his return in 1833, however, the focus of his social criticism fell heavily on America. If the European trilogy had interpreted feudal Europe by the standards of an American democrat, *Homeward Bound* and *Home as Found* (both 1838) present a picture of the United States seen through the eyes of an American gentleman fresh from Europe. Now Cooper attacks American vulgarity with the virulence of a Frances Trollope or a Dickens. And although still opposed to the "artificial" institution of hereditary aristocracy, he now places such emphasis on the folly of a provincial "public" in claiming equality with the "natural" gentleman of cosmopolitan training that his message invades the very American principles which he had earlier opposed to European facts. In *Home as Found* there is no room for the unqualified commitment to majority rule contained in the preface to *The Headsman*.

Cooper's attack on America was due partly to the influence of his long stay in Europe, partly to the changes which in the meantime had been wrought in America. Certainly it was, like his vision of Europe, an expression of his personality. He revealed his limitation when he wrote to a friend at home that he was not one of "those galloping gentry, who think the world is to be best understood in the market places."[20] For vigorous as his political response to Europe was, his vision was dimmed and his language clogged by theory. He was a systematic, but not a deep or subtle, thinker. And his sense of justice was much more developed than his understanding of men.[21] Europe therefore represented for him almost exclusively the evils of aristocratic "systems" of government exposed in his European novels, and the refinements of aristocratic society—of manners much more than of intellect—described at weary length in his travel books. With all his bellicose independence he illustrates, like Willis, an ambivalence which was typical of the American attitude toward Europe.

In particular, Cooper's theory of aristocracy was part of a traditional American distinction between an "artificial" aristocracy of birth and a "natural" aristocracy of worth, or talent, or merit, which goes back to John Adams and Jefferson and the eighteenth century and reaches forward into our own time. In the nineteenth century the concept was constantly resorted to. We have already seen it at work in Willis. In 1824 Emerson spoke in his *Journal* of "Nature's Gentlemen, who need no discipline, but grow straight up into shape and grace and can match the proudest in dignified demeanor and the gentlest in courtesy." In 1847, reporting from Italy to the New York *Tribune,* Margaret Fuller looked forward to a new Italy governed by "none but natural princes." In *Pierre,* Melville compared the "intensely artificial" political institutions of Europe with those of his own country, which seemed to him possessed of "the divine virtue of a natural law," and in *Moby Dick* he spoke of the "divine equality" of the "kingly commons." Thoreau and later Howells and Eliot of Harvard used the concept of natural nobility. It underlies Lowell's celebration of Lincoln in the Harvard Ode.[22] And James, after dramatizing it in *The American* with direct reference to the traditional social concept, finally transmuted it in his "heiress of all the ages" into an image of supreme spiritual beauty.

How deeply James was indeed rooted in the native tradition is suggested by other ties between him and the representative Cooper. Like Cooper, though more gently, James was to satirize the Irvingesque approach to England; like him, though with more sympathy for the American side, he was to contrast the artless independence of American girls with the cultivated restraint of their European sisters.[23] And if Cooper attributed to English society a heartless "sophistication without parallel," James was to picture it in *The Wings of the Dove*. But Cooper's preference for the "cold, dogged domination of English law"[24] over the more erratic tyranny of public opinion in free America was beyond James, for James lacked Cooper's social exclusiveness. The difference between the two is suggested in their attitudes toward social institutions and "manners." When James characterized the "thinly-composed society" of Hawthorne's America by its want of court, aristocracy, clergy, manors, abbeys, and other "items of high civilization," he was concerned with the needs of the novelist; in a somewhat similar passage Cooper was concerned with the needs of society itself. The American people, he said in *Home as Found*, "possess no standard for opinion, manners, social maxims, or even language"; they should therefore let themselves be guided by those among them who have had the advantage of associating with the more polished societies of Europe, just as "the inhabitants of the nursery" are guided by "the opinions of the drawing-room."[25] Of such paternalism James was incapable despite the fact that ultimately he came to think of "manners" as "the very core of our social heritage" and too precious to be flouted.[26] But manners to him were something more than patrician decorum. He knew too well how much conventions of behavior vary with time and place to make them an absolute index of right and wrong.

The differences between Cooper and James are indeed as significant as the similarities. Cooper's attack on American provincialism was itself tainted by the provincial snobbery which his contemporary Paulding scored when he said that the American "was always setting himself up for a fine gentleman" instead of being content to pass for the "honest and independent country farmer" that he "really was."[27] In 1894 James still pondered in his *Notebooks* "the eternal question of American snobbishness abroad." For the phenomenon persisted in a more blatant form. With the passing of the old agrarian America and the birth of a new money "aristocracy" after the Civil War, the hankering for the externals of European culture and for the amenities of an old "leisure class" flared up with a new vigor well stoked with funds. And this more rapacious form of the old appetite was to supply James with ample material for his international fiction.

And other attitudes and images persisted, and supplied James with subjects. The counterpart of social snobbery, the democratic image of a Europe paralyzed by lingering feudalism, seems in fact to have lived on even into our own time. In 1945, "a friendly and intelligent American officer" of World War II told the British historian Trevelyan that when he first came to England he expected to find "a land of castles with serfs tilling the soil for the benefit of a feudal aristocracy." Above all, Irving's romantic devotion to the "mementos" of history persisted—despite Bret Harte's assertion in 1868 that the "days of sentimental journeying" and of the "dear, old book of travel" with its "sentimental musings" were past. In one of his "London Letters" of 1885, George Smalley still speaks of a visit to Westminster as an American "pilgrimage" filled with a "rush of ancient memories." A year later, Holmes confesses that nothing is more "hackneyed than an American's description of his feelings in the midst of the scenes and objects he has read of all his days, and is looking upon for the first time."[28] And the language of the advertisements which the British Tourist Office even now places in American magazines, not to speak of the yearly summer rush of Americans to the Atlantic ports, continues the story.

That there might be a difference between the image and the reality, that the Europeans themselves at least thought so, is attested by the European reviews. Despite their varying points of view, despite their different political sympathies, one of their recurrent comments is that in their concern with various aspects of the lingering past Americans overlook the active European present, that their pictures of Europe are incomplete, that they consist of "fancies."[29] In the American reviews, on the other hand, such comments are conspicuously absent. American reviewers, to be sure, may share the romantic enthusiasm of Irving and his followers or endorse Cooper's democratic criticism; but they never note that the European takes his ruins for granted, that the tired laborer in the ivied church on Sunday thinks little of its storied past, and that English liberals may denounce aristocratic prerogatives more unequivocally than the republican magazine writer does. In short, they never note that nineteenth-century Europe, though rooted in the past, had a present too. And this silence bears witness once more to the bias of the American vision of Europe, to the "superstitious valuation" of Europe, as James called it.

In some of his early international fiction, James recognized and dramatized the bias of this vision as typically American, and this is one respect in which he is distinguished from his predecessors. But soon he began to analyze his own experience and, particularly, to draw conclusions from his observation of the conflict between American and European manners. And what most distinguishes him from earlier Americans is the gradual deepening of his perceptions. From surfaces and "superstitious" stereotypes of behavior his focus shifted to motives and causes. At first painting manners, he proceeded to analyze morals, and ended by creating his own image of Europe, richer and subtler than the earlier ones though still clearly the product of American eyes.

The moral criticism of Europe was of course no invention of James's. From the very beginning it had been implicit in the doctrine of the equality and the inalienable rights of men. Paine, for instance, spoke in *The Rights of Man* of the American government as "founded on a *moral theory.*" And in the preface to the *Columbiad* Barlow said that his purpose in the poem was "moral and political" since "the republican principle" was the foundation, not only of good government, but also of "all good morals." Conversely, Robert Coram in *Political Inquiries* (1791) had related the "wrong principles" of European government to the theory of natural depravity.[30] Cooper was to point out forty years later in *The Bravo* that by their "mockery" of the "sacred principles" of "truth and human justice" tyrannous and, therefore, "vicious" governments corrupted rulers and ruled alike—an idea directly related to the theory of "natural nobility."[31] Indeed, the whole question of the relative merits of the New World and the Old was originally tied to eighteenth-century ideas of nature by which Europeans rationalized their belief that in America man and beast alike were degenerating while Americans, needless to say, found evidence to prove the opposite.[32] One of Abigail Adams' always amusing and always charming letters may serve to illustrate the American view of the matter: "Do you know," she wrote from London in 1786, "that European birds have not half the melody of ours? Nor is their fruit half so sweet, nor their flowers half so fragrant, nor their manners half so pure, nor"—and here we return to the moral issue—"their people half so virtuous." Two years earlier in Paris she had been "disgusted" by the manners of Mme Helvetius, whom, had it had not been for Dr. Franklin's reassurances, she would have had to set down "for a very bad one, although sixty years of age, and a widow."[33]

Like the opposition to institutionalized aristocracy, the conviction that America was morally healthier than Europe was reinforced by the observation of the great gulf between the social classes in Europe. Jefferson noted in a letter from Paris in 1785 that "the great" were occupied by "intrigues of love" or, when they were too old for that, by intrigues of "ambition," while the mass of the people were suffering "physical and moral oppression." In these early American comments one finds repeatedly, moreover, the high cultivation of the arts balanced by a lack of moral cultivation on the part of men—not only of the elite, but also of the masses since, as Coram put it, the brutish ignorance of the "rabble" is the "natural parent of all enormity." And one finds this precarious state of affairs contrasted with "the tranquil, permanent felicity with which," in Jefferson's words, "domestic society in America blesses most of its inhabitants."[34]

Only rarely is this comparatively simple moral vision touched by hints of the complexity which was to be characteristic of James. An interesting passage occurs in the diary of John Adams under the date of June 2, 1778. After some reflections about the influence of Madame de Pompadour, the mistress of Louis XV, on the affairs of France, he asks himself: "Could there be any morality left" where "such examples were set up to the view of the whole nation?" The question and the reflections which it climaxes imply a moral condemnation, but Adams' answer to himself contains quite a different judgment: "Yes," he says. "There was a sort of morality. There was a great deal of humanity, and what appeared to me real benevolence. Even their politeness was benevolence. There was a great deal of charity and tenderness for the poor. There were many other qualities that I could not distinguish from virtues."[35] The significance of this and particularly of the last sentence for the reader of James is that Adams here points to different areas of moral behavior, condemning the public immorality which allowed a courtesan great influence over the affairs of the state and commending the personal virtue of benevolence and even politeness; condemning "licentiousness" and praising "charity and tenderness."

Adams here almost anticipates James's later views of the moral meaning of manners—almost, but not quite. For a century or so later James's dramatic analysis of a similar problem led to entirely different conclusions. He was to arrive at a point, finally, where he saw the moral contrast between America and Europe as part of a complex contrast of civilizations vitally affected by history. Of Strether, his hero in *The Ambassadors,* he said in his preliminary notes that he "imaginatively reconstructs" and "morally reconsiders" civilization. And this is exactly what James himself did —not merely in *The Ambassadors,* but progressively in a whole series of stories and novels. His method and his conclusions, as we shall see, were finally pragmatic. In 1778, however, the time was not ripe for pragmatism; and since Adams' judgments, like those of his contemporaries, were tied to eighteenth-century theories of reason and nature, the simultaneous presence of what to him were vice and virtue illustrated merely "the inconsistencies in the human character."[36]

The difference between Adams and James was the result of a century of scientific and philosophical as well as social change. When James began to write, the tranquil felicity of a predominantly agrarian society, which Jefferson had contrasted with the urban society of Paris, was disappearing rapidly—more rapidly and universally than the old gave way to the new in Europe. And the slower invasion of old tranquillities was one of the things which finally held James in Europe. For the sense of the past was no less strong in him than in the earlier Americans. But it was different. American writers of the first half of the century had seen the lingering past of Europe primarily as a matter either of the material "mementos"—the ruins, the monuments, the moss, and the ivy—or of political and social conservatism (the so-called feudal institutions) with its concomitant polish of manners. In James the lingering past became part of a stream of time extending into the present and accounting for it; in him the past lives, not only in outdated political institutions which ought to be dead or, vaguely, in the sentiments which romantic pilgrims allow themselves in the presence of its "mementos," but in the texture of society and of the active lives of individual men and women. Among the novelists preceding James only Hawthorne approaches this vision of the lingering European past to some degree, standing in this respect somewhere between James and such early writers as Irving or Cooper—perhaps as in *The Scarlet Letter* he stands between the seventeenth century of his ancestors and his own nineteenth. This is why the young James—not the old!—called him somewhat condescendingly "the last of the old-fashioned Americans."[37]

For, like Irving, Hawthorne still gave his warmest appreciation to the roots of European civilization at the expense of its contemporary and active forms; and like Cooper he could be a democratic critic. Yet he strongly differed from both. Unlike Irving, for instance, he abhorred pilgrimages to the shrines of great men because they never produced in him "the right feeling." And although he too realized that the "eager, almost childish interest in everything English" which he shared with his compatriots was in part owing to his early reading, this explanation was not enough for him. It is significant that when he tried to dramatize his sense of the relation between America and England he kept returning to the fable of the American claim to an English estate, which symbolizes a deeper and more compulsive attachment. In *Our Old Home* he speaks of the American affinity for England as "a sort of innate idea, the print of a recollection in some ancestral mind, transmitted, with fainter and fainter impress" through several generations but "reviving at every step" taken among the "hereditary haunts." In *Doctor Grimshawe's Secret,* the most nearly finished of his English fragments, the American claimant is propelled by exactly such affinities, "in some mysterious way latent in the depths of his character" and upon contact flaring again into a "deep yearning" of the "blood."[38]

But in Hawthorne, too, such yearnings were checked by an aversion to hereditary aristocracy. His attachment to democracy was, in fact, more solid than Cooper's. His democratic American in *Doctor Grimshawe* sees the injustice of the aristocratic system precisely in the fact that rank enables its holders to be really superior as men and to cultivate gracious "manners" at the expense of the common people.[39] One rather suspects that this American democrat would object to the pretensions of Cooper's "natural" gentleman of merit quite as much as to those of the hereditary English gentry. And indeed, Hawthorne had not a trace of snobbery in him. He rather seems to have taken social democracy for granted. To be sure, he could attribute American patriotism to "the singularity of our form of government"; in one of his preliminary notes he could even summarize the "great gist" of his English romance as "the natural hatred of men and the particular hatred of Americans to an aristocracy."[40] But in Hawthorne's context even such political formulations have moral overtones. And in the fragments of his English romance the American argument against England rests ultimately on the contrast between the vitality which America derives from her freedom from the weight and rut of tradition and, on the other hand, the torpor of England's bondage to a dying past.

This in itself foreshadows James's similar contrast between the moral spontaneity of Americans and the carefully cultivated manners of Europeans. But in *The Marble Faun,* where Hawthorne's moral preoccupation is thematically central, there are more anticipations. *The Marble Faun*—according to James "part of the intellectual equipment" of every "Anglo-Saxon visitor to Rome"[41]— may be described as a fable of the fall of man in which the part of Adam is played by a young Italian. His fall from Arcadian innocence is seen largely from the point of view of some American characters, and it is in part through them that Hawthorne expresses his sense of the contrast between the bleak but morally unencumbered prosperity of America and the aesthetically rich but morally heavy atmosphere of a Rome haunted by the "majestic and guilty shadows" of the past.[42] Yet Hawthorne's attitude toward Rome was deeply ambivalent. And if James finally ceased to draw a clear line between moral and aesthetic values, Hawthorne's failure to integrate the aesthetic background with the moral story of his Italian novel suggests at least an awareness of the tension between them. Whatever doubts about his moral inheritance Hawthorne had felt, at any rate, were increased by his submission to the aesthetic appeal of Europe. "We go all wrong, by too strenuous a resolution to go all right," he could comment in the essentially puritan *Marble Faun.*[43] And in the later *Doctor Grimshawe* the moral burden of the past, though certainly implied, is represented only in the shadowy legend of a bloody footstep.

London, Hawthorne later said in *Our Old Home,* had become for him the great city "of the Present," Rome the great city "of the Past," and in both he had "acquired a home-feeling" as "nowhere else in the world." James could have said this; to him London was "the biggest aggregation of human life—the most complete compendium of the world." And if he stayed, Hawthorne can be said to have almost stayed. After five years in Europe he had written to Ticknor: "I had rather be a sojourner in any other country than return to my own. The United States are fit for many excellent purposes, but they certainly are not fit to live in."[44] And as the date of his final return drew nearer, expressions of such doubts became more frequent. He had been abroad for a period of seven years, and no summer traveler knows how strongly seven years abroad pull at the roots a man has in his native soil.

Yet some sort of scruple kept Hawthorne from settling in Europe. He wanted to protect his children from similar uncertainties, and he still felt that America, if not the most "delightful," was at least "the healthiest and safest country to live in" and New England had less "mischief" in its atmosphere than any other spot on earth.[45] If Hawthorne can be described as a cosmopolitan prevented by his puritanism from becoming an expatriate, James was not thus prevented, though he always retained the puritan's moral concern. "Being a cosmopolite," he said in 1878, "is an accident, but one must make the best of it."[46] He did; and what he made of it is recorded in his work.

But his first responses to Europe, his earliest international stories as well as his early travel sketches, reflect many of the American attitudes traditional when he began to write. The English parts of the *Transatlantic Sketches* (collected in 1875) which he contributed to the *Nation* in 1872 are filled with romantic appreciations of "historical color," while at the same time they reveal an awareness of the dead hand of the past—not in Cooper's doctrinaire manner, but rather with something like Hawthorne's moral overtones. Thus James writes from Chester that the "beautiful scenic properties of English life" are peopled, not, as the American would like to think, "by the children of 'Merry England,' " but by the "victims of dismal old-world pains and fears." And he reflects that "packed away" behind the picturesque façades human life "can have expanded into but scanty freedom and bloomed into little sweetness." Such observations are far removed from Irving's tender melancholy; and indeed, when James indulged in a pilgrimage or in the play of "recollections" he was often aware of having fallen into the part of the "observant American" or of the "sentimental tourist," which meant the same thing.[47]

If England struck him as picturesque, Italy struck him even more so. But here, too, the eyes of the "magnanimous Yankee" were sometimes needed to transform, for example, some "miserable dwellings" in need of the attentions of an "enterprising board of health" into "the perfect felicity of picturesqueness." The public "letter" from Florence in which this particular passage occurs reminds one of Longfellow's similar but private one, and the fact that in 1873 James could exploit what forty years earlier would have spoiled Longfellow's "beautiful effusion" is indicative of the difference between the two writers and of the change in the public taste to which they appealed. And yet, in Italy James's enthusiasm was not easily broken. In 1869 he had spent his first day in Rome "reeling and moaning thro' the streets in a fever of enjoyment"— thus he described himself at the time. The simultaneous presence of all the ages since Roman times which Hawthorne had already been struck with, "all the Piazzas and ruins and monuments," made him feel that for the first time in his life he knew what the word *picturesque* meant.[48] For many years the spell of Italy remained so strong that at times James could, again somewhat like Hawthorne, feel it almost as "a nuisance and an importunity." And if in later years he lost some of his early love of traveling, if the barbarian hordes of Anglo-American and German tourists further deterred him, that first enchantment remained vivid all the same: in 1902, with a sidewise glance at all that Italy had meant to Goethe, he could congratulate a younger friend "on the great event of your young, your first, your never to be surpassed or effaced, prime Italiänische Reise."[49]

This partiality is reflected in the fact that of a total of nine stories which grew out of James's early trips to Europe in 1869-70 and 1872-74 five are laid in Italy. Some of them derive from literary sources,[50] others are thinly disguised travel sketches in which Americans, following more or less the route of James's own first approach to Italy, share his own sense of enchantment. But compared to James's later work they are strikingly conventional. The picture of Italy as the land of art, of passion, and of the survival of the pagan past conforms to traditional American images, and so does the undertone of social or political criticism contained in occasional allusions to the "heavy heritage" of the past, to the profligate alliance of "arts and vices,"[51] and to the daily misery of common people hidden behind the holiday show of the picturesque. True, these early stories contain hints of James's later concern with manners as well as of his later method; but the contrasts between American freedom and European conventionality—as in "At Isella" (1871) and *Roderick Hudson* (1875) —are not very original. And even the marriage motif—as in "The Last of the Valerii" (1874) and "Adina" (1874)—leads neither to psychological portraits of much subtlety nor to revealing comedy of manners since the foreign characters, Italians whose atavistic instincts are activated by relics of the antique past, remain close to the romantic stereotypes. In general in these early stories, the links between the scenic and the human aspects, their common reference to the survivals of antiquity, permits James little more psychological realism than Hawthorne achieved in *The Marble Faun.* This is more or less even true of *Roderick Hudson,* where a budding American artist is for his development quite as a matter of course removed from an aesthetically bleak New England to the rich beauty of Rome. As James recognized some thirty years later when he wrote the preface to that early novel, Italy—"so much more loved than one has ever been able, even after fifty efforts, to say!"—is not really "done" in that book.

About the time when James took up permanent residence in Europe in 1875 his interests took, however, a new turn marked clearly by the difference between the "Transatlantic Sketches" of 1872 to 1874 and the "Portraits of Places" which appeared in various magazines between 1876 and 1879 (collected 1883). In the "Portraits" James is concerned much more with people and less with scenery, art, and architecture than in the earlier "Sketches," and hence his attention to the picturesque falls off strikingly. He is now still more conscious of the difference between the points of view of the American traveler and of the native, between the American's typical "fondness for antiquity, his relish for picturesqueness, his 'emotional' attitude at historic shrines" and the native's unconsciousness of all these things. Moreover, he now realizes that "observation in any foreign land" is likely to be "extremely superficial," that his remarks about Italian gaiety, for instance, "may possibly be great nonsense"; that "half the time that we are admiring the brightness of the Italian smile the romantic natives may be, in reality, in a sullen frenzy of impatience and pain." Now he can feel that "there is something heartless in stepping forth into the streets of a foreign town to feast upon novelty when the novelty consists simply of the slightly different costume in which hunger and labor present themselves."[52]

Such notes in *Portraits of Places* are new, and a corresponding change has also come over James's fiction. Here his concern is now primarily with the conflict of manners and particularly with the attempts of Americans to adapt themselves to what they conceive to be European ways. Hence his concern with Europeanized Americans instead of Europeans as the antagonists of plain Americans. Hence also his attention to the snob, the "servile American," as Margaret Fuller had described him, who imitated European fashion and sought the acquaintance of "titled persons" in order to "win importance at home."[53] But what most distinguishes the James of this phase is that the traditional images of Europe, which his earliest stories still reflect, now become part of his subject matter. Now he begins to distinguish between the "Europe" in quotation marks, the "synthetic" product of the American imagination, and his own Europe, which is the result of a closer vision.

Finally, around the turn of the century, after the years devoted to drama and to purely English subjects, James returns to international contrasts. He himself said later that the internationalism of the great novels of this period was only "secondary,"[54] and so indeed it is, for he has now turned to an analysis of moral problems essentially independent of nationality. Yet in dramatizing moral distinctions, in searching for their causes, in allying them to the moral values of innocence and experience, he falls back on his old stage, where Americans and Europeans meet—so that, though "secondary," though only as a means to a more universal end, international contrast still figures in those late novels. The contrast of manners, too, still figures, particularly between the manners of a democratic society without "classes" and those of a society organized hierarchically. But the focus of the latest James differs radically from that of the earlier. For the comedy based on the conflict between American and European manners has now given way to the serious, sometimes tragic, problem piece, in which manners function as conventions determining morals.[55] The traditional American criticism of aristocracy as an institution, which entered James's earliest fiction, has disappeared too. Aristocracy now functions merely as a convention affecting the individual consciousness.

The focus, not on the physical action but on the individual awareness of it, on the "story of the story," is of course what has made James's late manner notorious. "Don't you think your style's a trifle affected?" he made one of his characters in *The Tragic Muse* ask another. And the answer may serve as a comment on his own development:

That's always the charge against a personal manner: if you've any at all people think you've too much [but] affectation must have begun, long ago, with the first act of reflective expression—the substitution of the few placed articulate words for the cry or the thump or the hug. Of course one isn't perfect: but that's the delightful thing about art, that there's always more to learn and more to do; it grows bigger the more one uses it and meets more questions the more they come up.[56]

The gradual refinement of James's own form was indeed inseparable from the increasingly complex questions it was designed to meet.

That there were more and more questions to meet and the cry or thump or hug served less and less for answer, was owing to his unusual opportunities. As a boy he had like other Americans fed on the English classics and on English magazines—supplemented in the cosmopolitan James household by the "great review," the *Revue des Deux Mondes*. But unlike most Americans, he had spent a large part of his youth in Europe, the first time "as a baby in long clothes,"[57] later as an adolescent. For four or five of his most impressionable years (1855 to 1860), with only a brief interlude at home, his father had led the family a nomads' life from Switzerland to England, France, Germany, from tutor to tutor, and from school to school, in order to give his children the kind of "sensuous education" which he believed America could not offer. Near the end of those years, in 1860, the young Henry wrote that the more he saw of the "estrangement of American youngsters from the land of their birth," the less he believed in it and that if they were to live in America, they ought to be brought up there too.[58] And he recalled the experience of these years much later in the preface to *The Reverberator* when he said that from as far back as he could remember he had carried in his side "the head of one of those well-directed shafts from the European quiver" to which "tender American flesh" used to be so "helplessly and bleedingly exposed."[59] In short, the father's insistence on an eclectic education had prepared the ground for both the love of *"contrasted* things" and the detachment from any one local sense of values which were to be characteristic of the son.

Something of this was doubtless in his mind in 1879 when in his book on Hawthorne James remarked that an American as "cultivated" as Hawthorne was would now inevitably be more "Europeanized," more "cosmopolitan."[60] At any rate, James's childhood trips to Europe were followed by others in 1869-70 and again in 1872-74, now as a young writer in search of experience, until in 1875 he settled there. What brought him to this decision can be traced in his letters, in his autobiographical books, even in his prefaces to the New York Edition. But in 1881, during the first of his brief visits home, he reviewed in his *Notebooks* the events, thoughts, impressions of the six years that had elapsed since his momentous decision, and since this record was meant for no other eyes than his own, it is not only more immediate but in a sense more trustworthy than his later accounts. Only a fragment of the passage need hold us here:

No European writer is called upon to assume that terrible burden [of choosing between America and Europe], and it seems hard that I should be. The burden is necessarily greater for an American—for he *must* deal, more or less, even if only by implication, with Europe; whereas no European is obliged to deal in the least with America.... The painter of manners who neglects America is not thereby incomplete as yet.[61]

In spite of the suggestion contained in the "as yet," the passage reveals once more the bias which has exposed James to the accusation of apostasy. He himself called his point of view *cosmopolitan*. This passage from the *Notebooks* makes it quite clear that the necessity to choose between America and Europe was, to James at least, a patently American fate. And indeed, in spite of the external circumstances of his life, his work remained deeply American. Yet without them, without his intimacy with the European and particularly the English scene, the detachment necessary for the fight against the "superstitious valuation of Europe" would have been impossible.

II The Middle Point of View

WHEN JAMES reread his international stories of the late 1870's in order to select some for the New York Edition, he confessed that the contrast between "the distinctively American and the distinctively European outlook" had always been extremely vivid for him.[1] In his later fiction its function might be secondary, but in the stories of those early years it was central. Highly conscious as he always was of his own art, he was quite right. For the conflict between these two distinctive points of view, seen from a middle point detached from either, is what characterizes many of the stories of those years.

His detachment from the American "superstitions" about Europe developed simultaneously with his dramatic method of narration. "The Last of the Valerii" (1874), for instance, is not simply the story of the marriage of an American girl to one of "those primitive" Italians. The generic description of the Italian as "the natural man," furnished with "nothing but senses, appetites, serenely luxurious tastes," indicates not so much what the Italian is like as how the American narrator at first sees him—very much as Hawthorne had seen the Donatello of his *Marble Faun*. And the story is concerned with how the narrator penetrates such American preconceptions. In one of his letters to the *Nation* of 1873 James had said that in general a traveler was "very likely to find a people" what he had "found them described to be under the mysterious woodcut in some Peter Parley task-book" of his childhood; but as we have seen, he soon realized that such observations were superficial, even nonsensical.[2] What the narrator of "The Last of the Valerii" learns in the course of the story he tells is something of this sort. James at first pictures him as something of a clever fool, for his story exemplifies the fight against the "superstitious valuation of Europe."

"The Last of the Valerii" is, however, by no means the first story in which the definition of a point of view is thematically important. Already in "The Madonna of the Future" (1873) certain problems of the artist are dramatized by means of three contrasting points of view: the first is represented by an American aspirant who, having Raphael's "brain" but not his "hand," dreams away his life in front of an untouched canvas, convinced that he is doomed to failure because as an American he is "excluded from the magic circle" of art; the second is that of another American, a lady of the Anglo-American colony in Florence who cultivates "the dignity of a social high-priestess of the arts," without knowing much about them; and the third is that of a practical Italian who employs his manual aptitude in turning out unbreakable but suggestive figurines of cats and monkeys illustrating "the different phases" of what the narrator delicately calls "the amorous advance and the amorous alarm." The tale is highly ironic, and it should be obvious that none of these characters speak for the author. If James's voice can here be heard at all, it must be from the lips of a fourth character, the narrator, who is detached and amused by the pathetic comedy even if in the end he cannot withhold his sympathy from the frustrated American Raphael because he sees him as one of "the famished race."

With the still earlier "A Passionate Pilgrim" (1871) we turn to James's first English story, in fact the only English story he wrote before he settled in Europe. "A Passionate Pilgrim" and "The Madonna of the Future" are structurally similar, and in the New York Edition James indeed grouped them together. "A Passionate Pilgrim" is the story of an American claimant to an English estate, a fable symbolizing the traditional home-feeling for England which Hawthorne had expressed in *Our Old Home* and in *Doctor Grimshawe,* his own fragmentary romance of such a claim. One must again beware of identifying James with the sickly, feverish hero, who feels that America is exile and whose only wish, now that he is on the point of dying, is to be at least buried "in some English churchyard, beside some ivied tower, beneath an old gnarled black yew." Again James's own point of view is rather that of the narrator, a more or less objective register of events like the narrator of "The Madonna of the Future." The relation between narrator and hero is in fact strikingly similar in the two stories. In both the hero represents the extreme of agitated worship of cultural symbols which he misses in his own country; in both this worship is linked with a state of mind obviously pathological; in both this state of mind arouses the curiosity, even the qualified sympathy, of the American narrator, who views it as in all but its morbidness characteristic of his countrymen. Thus in "A Passionate Pilgrim" he speaks of "the latent preparedness" of Americans for the "characteristic features of English life," of its origins "in the soil of our early culture." But constantly the English scene reminds him, too, of his childhood reading in "the British classics," and the coffee room at the Red Lion in London, for instance, stirs him to considerable depths of emotion because he saw it years ago at home in Illinois, "in books, in visions, in dreams, in Dickens, in Smollett, in Boswell."

In one of the prefaces written for the New York Edition more than thirty years later, James made "A Passionate Pilgrim" and "The Madonna of the Future" the occasion of a backward glance at his own state of mind in the early 1870's. He recalled the "unnatural precosity" with which, in 1869, he had taken to Europe as a result of his early exposure in childhood. And his "brace of infatuated 'short stories'" struck him in retrospect as highly "documentary" of the nostalgia he had felt after his return to America in 1870.[3] But such remarks explain the two stories only in part. The prefaces are an attempt at tracing "his whole operative consciousness," taking "his whole unfolding, his process of production, for a thrilling tale,"[4] and it is not to be expected that his remounting of "the stream of composition," as he liked to describe the process, resulted in a wholly objective record. Indeed, a "Passionate Pilgrim" contains a note radically opposed to the nostalgic. The British system of primogeniture, which on the one hand has created the charming English country places admired by romantic American pilgrims, on the other hand comes in for democratic criticism when an impoverished younger son is forced to emigrate to America, where society promises to be kinder to him. In the ferocity, moreover, with which the English country gentleman defends his property against the American claimant, in his ruthless disregard for justice, there is a note of the sinister. So that even if the nostalgic note outweighs the critical, "A Passionate Pilgrim" illustrates the characteristic ambivalence of the American relation to Europe.

How much this was a matter of the conscious use of convention becomes clear when the story is compared with James's letters and notes of this period. Contrast, for instance, the admiration of the narrator of "A Passionate Pilgrim" for the Red Lion in London with James's own reaction to Morley's Hotel: "I think I was never so gloom-smitten" as the first night "at Morley's," he wrote home early in March of 1869; "the tortuous passages—the dingy musty bedroom—the two penny candle—the stupid coffee-room." Happily, like Dickens, Smollett, Boswell? Not a bit; painfully, rather, "like a story in an old magazine at the dentist's." Yet, James's remark in *The Middle Years* (1917), the last fragment of his "autobiography," that on his first adult visit to England the pleasure of "recognition" was for months "the liveliest principle at work" was not entirely a distortion of the early James by the late. His letters suggest that if he was not always the passionate pilgrim, he could at least assume the role without doing violence to himself. In March, 1870, for instance, he speaks of a walk through "elm-scattered meadows and sheep-cropped commons" and past "ivy-smothered dwellings"—a region so filled "with all things suggestive of the opening chapters of half-remembered novels, devoured in infancy" that he felt as if he were "pressing all England" to his soul. In London seven years later he is still conscious of moving "on identified ground."[5]

About the British people, too, his feelings were mixed from the start. Their stolidity could annoy him, and in the women in particular a "deathly want" of "intellectual grace," of "moral spontaneity," as he tentatively called the qualities which were to be characteristic of his later American girls. Thus in 1870. In 1878, society at a country house, though "one of the ripest fruits of time," strikes the "cosmopolitanized American" as insuperably flat. From the beginning he could condemn and praise in one breath: "Considering that I lose all patience with the English about fifteen times a day," he wrote in 1880, "I get on with them beautifully and love them well," for "taking them all together they are more complete than other folk, more largely nourished, deeper, denser, stronger." And similarly, his condemnation of English women in 1870 ends with a retraction of "all those brutalities about the Engländerinnen. They are," James concludes, "the mellow mothers and daughters of a mighty race."[6]

This complex reaction, reflected also in *Transatlantic Sketches*, does not in the least mean that James was uncertain of his feelings about the English. He would have been less human had he been more of one mind. His private review of this period of his life in 1881 in his *Notebooks* reveals how irresistibly Europe, and England in particular, attracted him. "My choice is the old world—

my choice, my need, my life." He recalls how in 1874 he felt it his duty to try living at home, how he returned "with very loyal intentions" only to find that America was not for him. And as his reminiscences continue it becomes clear that the year spent in Paris from October, 1875, to November, 1876, was merely a station on his almost inevitable course to England and London—England with its "delicious old houses" on the soil "over which so much has passed and out of which so much has come," with its "accumulations of expression, of tone," and where one's thoughts turn to the stories and dramas "of all the life of the past"; and London, with its fog, its dirt, its ugliness (the list is much longer); dreary, stupid, vulgar—all this and more—but magnificent, "the biggest aggregation of human life—the most complete compendium of the world."[7]

This ardent self-confession and its more moderate echoes in the letters, private and public, show that "A Passionate Pilgrim"— for we must now briefly return to that story—is not out of accord with James's state of mind at the time of composition. Yet, it is not simply a reflection of personal nostalgia. Describing it in the preface to the New York Edition as a sop "instinctively thrown to the international Cerberus," James recalls that in writing it he wished his "ground-stuff" to be "as American as possible, and even to the pitch of fondly coaxing it."[8] This means that quite consciously he made "A Passionate Pilgrim" into a characteristic American fable, contrasting two major American reactions toward Europe. Hence the social and political criticism of aristocracy, which goes back to the very beginnings of the American republic but is strikingly lacking in James's personal writings, where his strictures on the English focus entirely on character but not on institutions. Hence also the figure of the dispossessed heir as a symbol of American nostalgia. For although James could share the nostalgia, the symbol was not original with him. The figure of the American claimant had achieved something resembling the status of a literary convention. N. P. Willis had used it as a device for contrasting English and American society;[9] Hawthorne had used it in his fragmentary English romance for purposes very similar to James's; and Mark Twain was to make it the object of his burlesque humor in *The American Claimant*. Moreover, the literary figure had its origins in reality: in *Our Old Home* (1863) Hawthorne recalled how as consul in Liverpool he was frequently approached by Americans with pretensions to English property, a fact James showed himself aware of when in his book on Hawthorne he spoke of these odd petitioners.

James's early treatment of France differs significantly from his treatment of Italy and England. If Italy functions in his early stories as a land of art and the picturesque, England as a shrine for cultural pilgrims or as an object lesson in the social injustice of hereditary aristocracy, "Madame de Mauves" (1874) and *The American* (1876-77) form their image of France largely in terms of a contrast between French and American character. In this they point forward to the concern characteristic of the later James, although the conception of French character in terms largely of a conventional stereotype is something that could satisfy only the early James.

Comparison with "A Passionate Pilgrim" yields another definition of the transitional nature of these two French tales. Like that early English story, they contain a criticism of aristocracy; but whereas in "A Passionate Pilgrim" it is primarily social and political, primarily of aristocracy as an institution, in "Madame de Mauves" and *The American* it is moral. This is particularly pronounced in "Madame de Mauves," where James already uses the marriage formula characteristic of so much of his international drama. The contrast here is between two entirely different bases of morality—between the individual conscience of a young American girl and the voice of the "confessional" which in France is necessary to curb "the whisper of opportunity." The contrast and the conflict are between what amounts to the integrity of American idealism and an opportunistic French realism which inevitably

strikes the American as corrupt. James was to draw a similar contrast almost thirty years later in *The Ambassadors,* though he eval-
uated it differently, less superstitiously, as he might have said; and
it is typical of this early stage of his development that what
"Madame de Mauves" emphasizes is less the fundamental philosophical distinction than the American bias in the picture of France.
If a secondary theme and with it a certain ambiguity in the moral
evaluation of the heroine's conduct are at least dormant in this story,
the same is not true of *The American,* a more ambitious but also
more conventional picture of the same contrast.

In *The American* the moral contrast after all is tied to the
contrast between two social and political systems. Christopher
Newman, James's hero in the full sense of the word, is not only
the representative American, the new man; he is also the "heir
of all the ages"—to use James's later formulation. Early in the
novel, he is described as "the great Western Barbarian, stepping
forth in his innocence and might" to gaze "at this poor corrupt
old world." But this is not the way he sees himself. "I have the
instincts," he says, "if I haven't the forms of a high old civilisation,"
and his story is quite literally presented as the proof of it. Newman
undergoes a test: cruelly wronged by a family of French aristocrats "pretending to represent the highest possible civilisation and
to be of an order in every way superior to his," he obeys, in the
words of James's preface, "one of the large and easy impulses
generally characteristic of his type" and foregoes revenge.[10] This
magnanimity, the sign of his civilized instincts, is foreshadowed
early in the novel when he explains that the idea of passing by a
similar opportunity of just revenge in his business career became
for him "the one thing" to save his "life from a sudden danger."
The danger was the moral danger inherent in a life directed
entirely toward the uninhibited acquisition of money, and the fact
that the episode is wholly unnecessary for the progress of the
action emphasizes its significance for Newman's character and
thereby for the theme of the novel. The sacrifice of revenge and

gain has been the turning point in Newman's career, for he is
not the average American. His type, the type of which his magnanimity is *"generally* characteristic"—the italics are James's own
—represents the best in America. Newman is "one of nature's
noblemen," and his story, quite in the American tradition, dramatizes a competition between his "natural" nobility and the "artificial" nobility of his French antagonists. The prize is the title of
representing the morally "highest" civilization.[11]

To describe the European system as artificial is of course to
proclaim it as the loser, and James, true to his origin, does exactly
that. If magnanimity is the mark of nature's nobleman, pretense
is the mark of artificial aristocrats. They assert that the marriage
of their daughter to a "commercial person" is incompatible with
their high traditions, but in the very act of doing so prove their
speciousness: because the Bellegardes covet Newman's millions,
they have first pledged their honor not to obstruct his suit, only
to break their word as soon as he has won the daughter's love.
The first half of the novel, which comes to an end with this
betrayal of their confessed principles, is devoted to polishing the
hard brilliance of the picture of their urbanity, a quality underlined
by the name of the *chef de famille*—Urbain. The second half cen-
ters on what the polished surface hides: in trying to get to the
bottom of their sudden reversal, Newman discovers abysses of
criminal enormity—the coercion of the daughter by means only
the uglier for being left vague, and the murder of the husband by
the wife with an acquiesence of the son amounting almost to parri-
cide. Admittedly, such a summary makes no attempt to understate
the melodrama, but neither does it exaggerate; and the melodrama
underlines—as it is likely to do in the early James—the conventional
simplicity of the international contrast.

If the force of melodrama serves to drive home beyond mistake
the speciousness of the aristocratic claim to superior civilization,
melodrama is nevertheless not the whole of *The American*. The
picture of French hypocrisy as long as hypocrisy serves, of French

cynicism when pretense is no longer effectual, is corroborated on a lower social level and in a lower key by the Nioches, father and daughter—the latter a determined little damsel climbing the social ladder by a competent barter of her God-given graces, the former volubly asserting his respectability while living on the profits of her trade. Count Valentin, the youngest of the Bellegardes but Newman's friend, rather admires the determination of Mlle Nioche: though she may not differ from the average as far as mere ambition goes, he says, her "resolution and capacity" are exceptional; clearly she is "one of the celebrities of the future," and success after all "justifies everything."[12] Valentin is merely frivolous; but although harmless, although in fact himself "the soul of honor," he pays with his life when his admiration of the practical Mlle Nioche lands him in a duel. The lesson has been expensive for him, but he has bravely learned it. On his deathbed he makes Newman a solemn and abject apology for the shame of "the ancient house of Bellegarde," for the name which once *was* noble.

In the winter of 1906 to 1907, when he reviewed a number of his early pieces for the New York Edition, James was struck with what seemed to him a lack of realism in the picture they presented of Europe. He made the preface to *The American* in particular the occasion of an extended discussion of the differences between realism and romance, because in rereading this most sustained achievement of his early phase after so many years he found to his surprise that what it represented was experience "uncontrolled by our general sense of 'the way things happen,'" the kind of experience "which romance alone more or less successfully palms off on us." Yet at the same time he recalled with amusement that in writing *The American* he had thought he was "acutely observing—and with a blest absence of wonder at its being so easy."[13] What he recalled was, in other words, a certain ingenuousness in the face of the European scene which he had shared with other American writers and which explains in part why his early stories portray Europe so much in terms of American stereotypes.

The definition of "the real" and "the romantic" which the mature James formulates in this preface—quite apart from our accepting or rejecting it as a definition of those terms—is a revealing comment not only on *The American* but on other American treatments of Europe. "The real," James says, "represents to my perception the things we cannot possibly *not* know, sooner or later, in one way or another"; the "romantic stands, on the other hand, for the things that, with all the facilities in the world" we "never *can* directly know; the things that can reach us only through the beautiful circuit and subterfuge of our thought and our desire." If *The American* struck the later James as romantic, the reason therefore was that it represented not directly known reality but something vitally colored by his own mind. Strictly speaking, James's distinction is of course specious, since all perceptions are the result of an interaction between subject and object, are colored by the perceiving mind. But for us the particular value of his formulation lies in its emphasizing the subjective element in his and other early American images of Europe, in its emphasizing so pointedly the contribution made to these images by the "circuit and subterfuge" of the American imagination.

In *The American,* then, the later James recognized an example of an unconscious American distortion. In the stories and novels which followed it this distortion is a major thematic concern, and this change of focus marks a major step in James's progress from a strictly American toward what he called a cosmopolitan point of view. He came to make conscious use of certain traditional American attitudes which he had begun by reflecting unconsciously—came to use them as part of the motivation of his American characters. If the author of *The American* had been "romantic," he now turned to portraying his American characters as entertaining "romantic" notions about Europe, as being under the spell of an American image, "the 'Europe'—synthetic symbol!—of the American mind," as he later phrased it.[14] Needless to say, this means that James's own attitude toward America and Europe was changing. But he did not simply substitute English for American loyalties. If in point of view he detached himself from the country of his birth, he remained detached from the country where he lived as well, and the fact is reflected in his fiction. For his central theme in this phase of his career involved not only American misconceptions of Europe. It often involved also a mutual misunderstanding between Americans and Europeans, dramatized through their failure to achieve satisfactory relations with each other.

In *The American,* however, James is still much more American than cosmopolitan. To be sure, he is capable of the objectivity of satire, as he shows in the incidental sketch of a New England minister, traveling on funds supplied by his flock in order that he may enrich his mind with the treasures of European art but constantly prevented from doing so by his high moral seriousness, which will not let him abandon himself to enjoyment of that art. New England reverberates whenever the Rev. Babcock opens his mouth. But if this indicates James's ironic detachment from one American type, Babcock and the grave emphases of his homilies—"*do* remember that Life and Art *are* extremely solemn"—merely serve to underline Newman's easy magnificence. And if Newman's attempt to marry a Bellegarde turns out to have been ill advised, his failure is not the result of self-delusion, for the woman herself quite justifies his high expectations. It is entirely the result of the melodramatic villainy of the mother and brother, of a wickedness too deep to foresee. All of which merely heightens James's emphasis on his "superlative American" and thereby on the "romantic" burden of the novel.

This is highlighted by a contrast not only with the stories which followed *The American* but even with "Madame de Mauves," which preceded it by a couple of years. Both these novels are laid in France, and in both Americans are victimized by a social order which supposes itself superior to theirs. But while *The American,* for the sake of contrasting two opposed concepts of civilization, emphasizes the nobility of its hero, "Madame de Mauves" raises a question about American idealism. To be sure, in its own words, it is the "miserable story of an American girl, born to be neither slave nor toy, marrying a profligate Frenchman, who believes that a woman must be one or the other." But the heroine's fate is largely the result of her own romantic delusions. Just because her imagination is of "radical purity," just because she is "profoundly incorruptible," she is more inclined to believe in "fables" as long as they have "a certain nobleness of meaning" than in "well-attested but sordid facts." And since a widowed mamma, "fonder of Homburg and Nice than of letting out tucks in the frocks of a vigorously growing daughter," has had her educated in a Parisian convent, a place stimulating her susceptibilities and at the same time protecting them from the fresh air of reality, she has come to cherish "a romantic belief that the best birth is the guaranty of an ideal delicacy of feeling." The story of her marriage to the French Baron de Mauves, like Newman's story, proves that the "best birth" is nothing of the kind. But unlike Newman, she has only herself to blame if the lesson is painful—herself for her native sentimentalism and her mamma for sowing the seeds of her conceits. It is no accident that her name is Euphemia.

James calls them "pernicious conceits," and though it is veiled in ambiguity, his criticism takes on a sharper note. For Euphemia is not the only sufferer. Moved finally by her steadfast virtue, the baron reforms—only to find that with continued steadfastness she refuses to forgive him; whereupon, in despair, he blows out his brains. If he has done her justice, she has done him not a whit more, and we do not quite know whether to admire or to shrink from a purity which appears to be so incorruptible as to deny all compassion.

Nor are we quite sure of James's final touch. The story is seen almost entirely through the eyes of Longmore, a young American who meets Euphemia in her dejection, sympathizes with her, and falls in love with her. It is ultimately the story not so much of Euphemia's fate as of the gradual growth of Longmore's understanding. And the crisis of *their* relations comes when she refuses his offer to save her from the baneful incongruity of her marriage, refuses because it would taint them both with the very corruption from which he intends to save her. After this the last few pages are devoted entirely to Longmore: he returns to America, morally uplifted by a sense that in "conceiving an ideal of conduct for him" Euphemia has offered him an opportunity for emulating a moral beauty which far surpasses the physical beauty he wanted to possess. But when the story closes on the statement that Longmore, on receiving the report of the baron's end, has lost his appetite to marry her now that she is free, because his tenderness has been chilled by "a feeling for which awe would be hardly too strong a name," we flounder in Jamesian ambiguity. Longmore's awe seems akin to the uncertainty we ourselves have felt. Is Euphemia's incorruptible consistency divine or inhuman? Is Longmore's aloofness an expression of humility or of fright? James's very wording seems calculated to emphasize the question. But when we remember the sources of Euphemia's virtue, we wonder whether the final note of Longmore's withdrawal is not a token of the author's own dissociation from her "idealism." For planted by a mother fonder of European romance than of American reality, and in the seclusion of a nunnery nurtured, as James says, on "ultramontane works of fiction" and the "perfumed gossip" of young ladies, it differs after all from the "idealism" of Don Quixote only by being less appealing.

Yet "Madame de Mauves" is nevertheless the first of James's many tales of American disenchantment. It dramatizes the contrast between two visions of Europe—the romantic and the real, the sentimental and the objective—one of which, Euphemia's, is presented explicitly as an American mirage, an example of the modern vulgarization of the image of Europe created by the American romantic tradition. But what James opposes to this as European "reality" is also an American vision because, deriving from another American tradition—that of the democratic indictment of lingering feudalism—it too purports to represent the whole by focusing on a part. All this means that "Madame de Mauves" is transitional, that its author had objectified only a part of his American point of view, a fact reflected in the preface to the New York Edition: here James groups "Madame de Mauves" with "A Passionate Pilgrim" among his early "artless" fables but suggests that, since it was written in Europe, it was without the nostalgic note.[15] Yet, already the young American girl is the central figure of James's international drama; already he dramatizes morality in terms of the implications of knowledge and ignorance; so that "Madame de Mauves" points across the whole of his career to his latest novels.

As we have seen, however, the moral contrast underlying this early story as well as *The American* is conceived almost in black and white: a highly idealized American virtue doing honorable battle with what is almost a caricature of aristocratic villainy. Even the ambivalence of the portrait of Euphemia is no denial of this, since whatever makes us feel uneasy in her presence is simply the glare of a whiteness too blinding for human eyes—a whiteness which, like Melville's, is the ambiguous source of metaphysical awe. But James was not a metaphysician. He was much closer to Hawthorne than to Melville, and when after reading *Pragmatism* he wrote to William that he had "unconsciously pragmatised" all his life,[16] he described accurately his method of analyzing moral problems.

For central as the question of morality is, not only in his international fiction but in most of his later fiction as well, it is inseparable from the analysis of human motives. And since he was acutely aware of the relation of conduct to convention, his psychological analysis of motives was inseparable from his concern with manners, the concern which underlies the famous passage in his *Hawthorne* deploring the handicap which the "terrible denudation" of America—a country with "no court, no personal loyalty, no aristocracy, no church, no clergy, no army, ... no museums, no pictures, no political society, no sporting class—no Epsom nor Ascot!"—constituted for a novelist.[17] How important to the work of a novelist, as opposed to a romancer, James considered these paraphernalia of "high civilization" is made clear by a letter to Howells, who in reviewing James's *Hawthorne* had protested against the proposition that "it takes an old civilization to set a novelist in motion." "It is on manners, customs, usages, habits, forms, upon all these things matured and established, that a novelist lives— they are the very stuff his work is made of," James rejoined; and in asserting that in the absence of these "we have simply the whole of human life left," Howells, to James's mind, was begging the question, since just so much less of it was left as these same paraphernalia represented—and, James added, "they represent an enormous quantity."[18]

Such convictions indicate the direction his own work was to take, though the emphasis which it derived from them did not always remain the same. As prolonged residence abroad made the superficial differences between American and European manners familiar and therefore less absorbing to him, he turned for a time from the international scene to purely English subjects, gradually lowering his sights at the same time from the surface of the world of manners to more hidden currents of ethical feeling—a focus which he retained when toward the turn of the century his native interest in the American character reasserted itself. From this later vantage point he saw Hawthorne differently, saw him as a proof "that an American could be an artist, one of the finest, without 'going outside' about it." Hawthorne, in fact, he could finally feel, "had become one just by being American *enough*."[19] Thus he wrote at a time when his own novels, outgrowing the strict limits of realism, had taken on the form, if not of "romances" in the sense in which Hawthorne had used the term, yet of fables of the inner life which depend less on the multiplicity of external detail than the young aspirant to realism had felt desirable. And yet, if he could rest even those more deeply searching novels firmly on a framework of manners accurately observed, this was possible only because he had familiarized himself with those manners by more than passive observation, because he had put them into active use in the international stories of his early European years. A few months before the first instalment of *The American* appeared in the *Atlantic Monthly,* James established himself permanently in London, and his fiction took the new turn toward an increasingly objective portrayal of the conflict of manners. The variety of the aspects of this conflict gives the stories dramatizing them in fact almost the appearance of a collection of data. One of them must here serve as an illustration.[20]

"An International Episode" (1878-79) is the classic example of James's dramatization of the mutual misunderstanding of Americans and Europeans. It still reflects some of the traditional American views of the differences between a democratic and an aristocratic society, but these differences are here not his major subject. The story is based on a conflict of visions: between two American visions of England—a romantic and a skeptical one—and between two English visions of America, similarly differentiated. It would be a tragedy of innocence if it were not a comedy of the errors of pseudo sophistication. It is a story specifically of the period after the Civil War, which James later recalled ironically as a time when "introductions, photographs, travellers' tales and other aids to knowingness" were the mark of the American traveler in Europe.[21] The contrast between the folly of this "knowingness" and the wisdom of an earlier romantic innocence is implicit in "An International Episode"—only, we must add, with the ironic barbs cutting East as well as West.

James's impartiality is reflected in the symmetrical structure of the story. It begins in America, where Bessie Alden, a young American girl, and Lord Lambeth, a young English nobleman, meet and, immediately interested in each other, plan to meet again in England. Bessie's older sister, Mrs. Westgate, however, whose representative type James establishes from the start by filling her social patter—pages of it!—with all the American clichés about the differences between the two countries,[22] does what she can to protect Bessie from disappointment. Upon their arrival in London, where the second half of the story takes place, she tells her a lurid "travellers tale" to prove what every up-to-date American knows: that English noblemen repay American hospitality habitually by snubs and outright insult. And when Bessie refuses to believe her, all she can do is commiserate with the "poor, sweet child," as she keeps calling her. For Mrs. Westgate is past that "primitive stage" of culture when Americans expressed their romantic sense of England's greatness by pilgrimages to historical monuments; she has graduated to the higher sophistication of those Americans who, fully alive to the importance of social matters, will neither forget their democratic dignity nor let anybody suspect the slightest gap in their familiarity with aristocratic etiquette. Hence, "following the fashion of many of her compatriots," she conforms minutely with all its requirements while at the same time, thanks to her vigilant watch for signs of English condescension, forgetting not infrequently her own good manners. Always on the defense, she can be discourteously aggressive—a fact which, typically, Englishmen note in her as typical of American women. Above all, however, she harasses Bessie with a protectiveness no less ungenerous than unnecessary since Lord Lambeth, with not a speck of snobbery or guile, ends quite simply by proposing.

Bessie's refusal of him knocks the last nail in the coffin of Mrs. Westgate's sophistication, for now she is driven to admit that, despite her democratic pretensions to the contrary, not to become allied to the English aristocracy is disappointing. It also cuts, however, with sharp irony through the fog of English notions. Just as Bessie is chaperoned by her sister, so Lord Lambeth by his cousin, Percy Beaumont, thereto appointed by Lambeth's mamma. Like Mrs. Westgate, Beaumont is the knowing one of the pair, "the man of talent," "the clever man," as James keeps ironically calling him. *He* is highly conscious of what is common *English* knowledge: that naturally American girls are out to hook an English lord. We are not there to see his face when he hears of Bessie's refusal, but we may assume that his reaction is not unlike that of the British reviewer who was indignant at the impudence of James's imagining the situation.

That the English should have taken this story amiss surprised James. He felt that he had been "very delicate,"[23] and indeed this tragicomedy of innocence ground in the mill of convention is more subtly ironic than may appear at first glance. But if it plays with equal irony over the foibles of the two nations, it is almost as impartial in its praise. For if Bessie is a compliment to American women, Lambeth is no mean portrait of an English lord. Perhaps it is not saying very much for him that he appreciates Bessie, though it is significant that he likes her for the very self-reliance which we, too, admire and—more important—of which he has his own share. But what James means to emphasize are of course the qualities by which he is distinguished from his hidebound foil— his modesty, his gaiety, and above all his openness to the world. Always ready for adventure and experiment, though typically he speaks of them as mere "larks," he is the opposite of the stereotype of the stuffy lord. And yet, he does not come up to Bessie's expectations. In part, her refusal is motivated by democratic pride, but it has a deeper cause than that.

For likable as the young man is, he has the misfortune of being a "hereditary legislator," as much to his embarrassment she keeps telling him, and therefore, *properly* should be "a great mind—a great character." This he is not, and nobody knows it better than himself. He is on the contrary simply a very nice young man, which is what after all attracts her to him, but of a modesty which, while commending him to the reader, is fatal to his chances with Bessie. For Bessie, good American romantic that she is, has formed her own image of England, so that what she expects in going there—and James means us to note the Irvingesque vocabulary of this key passage—are charming "associations," the pleasure of resting her eyes on "the things she had read about in the poets and historians," mementos of the past and "reverberations of greatness." What she unfortunately expects of Lord Lambeth in particular is that "he would be an unconscious part of the antiquity, the impressiveness" of England and, over and above this, an authority on English history —imputations, all of these, which now amuse him, now bore him, now embarrass him, but which above all he denies by deed and word with disarming candor. Alas, he is only too unconscious; he refuses to reverberate.

Whether James's irony points more at Lambeth's simplicity or Bessie's unreasonable expectations is perhaps an academic question. But remembering *Vanity Fair* and the great Lord Steyne, we cannot help suspecting a motive behind James's repeated references to Thackeray as the particular source of Bessie's exalted notions of nobility. And when he tells us that for a young man in Lambeth's position—though the young man dislikes talking about *that* and usually changes the subject—she has conceived an "ideal of conduct," the striking verbal echo reminds us of Euphemia de Mauves, another victim of romantic illusions about nobility. The difference between that story and this is of course that there is no doubt whatever about James's sympathy with Bessie. Nor, for that matter, with Lord Lambeth. For while he is the victim of her illusions, they are both victims of a world so deeply entangled in international prejudice as to make a simple human relationship impossible, a world whose ignorance differs from theirs only by being snobbish instead of gracious, suspicious instead of trusting, small and fatuous instead of generous.

But such a summary overstates the moral tone of this story. For it is essentially a comedy of the international conflict of manners, and whatever moral discriminations it suggests are not—as in "Madame de Mauves" or *The American*—between a democratic and an aristocratic society, but between types common to both. This detachment from any one national point of view is what characterizes James's stories of this period, and the result of these exercises—for though some achieve a high polish others are just that—was that when his interest in international differences later reasserted itself, his discriminations were deepened and refined. From that later perspective "An International Episode" and its companion pieces, "The Pension Beaurepas" (1879), "A Bundle of Letters" (1879), "The Siege of London" (1883), struck him as museum pieces, at best archaic subjects "treated by a 'primitive' master of high finish." And yet, even in those later years of *The Ambassadors* and *The Wings of the Dove* he could produce what he called an occasional "stray spark of the old 'international' flame."[24]

These late stories, too, deal on the whole more with American images of Europe than with Europe itself. The story called " 'Europe' " (1899), for instance, deals with no Europe outside the minds of its characters, hence the quotation marks belonging to the title.[25] It dramatizes the morbid perversity of a mother's idea that the old world is a mere storehouse of "food for conversation" by contrasting it with the late fulfilment, the "rich ripe *seconde jeunesse*" one of her spinster daughters finds there. In "Flicker-bridge" (1902) the old romantic American delight in a dreamy old English country house comes in conflict with the strident vulgarity of modern journalism, which threatens to destroy the thing it cele-brates.[26] "The Beldonald Holbein" (1901), a more complicated comedy, begins with the contrast between two kinds of beauty, that of Lady Beldonald, who looks "as if she took out every night her large lovely varnished eyes and put them in water," and that of plain Mrs. Brash, imported to London from America to act as foil to the younger woman. With a face "in which every wrinkle" is "the touch of a master," Mrs. Brash, however, turns out to be a perfect Holbein; and when Lady Beldonald jealously ships her back where she came from, she soon dies because her triumph in "superior sophisticated" London has unfitted her for living unappre-ciated among the "children of darkness"—with which the "old 'international' flame" begins to flicker in the unquiet air of irony. For while the " 'aesthetic' perceptive 'European' 'air,' " as with a flurry of suggestive quotation marks James tells himself in his

preliminary notes,[27] is necessary to awaken in Mrs. Brash a sense
of her own beauty, this beauty itself is a product of "unenlightened"
America which all the creams of London cannot match.

If in some of these late stories the international is merely a
means to the treatment of a more central theme, one of them, however, comes close to being another "International Episode," and for
that reason is a measure of certain changes in James's emphasis
between 1878 and 1900. "Miss Gunton of Poughkeepsie" (1900)
is again the story of an international marriage which, because of a
collision of manners, never comes off. The crisis in the engagement
of Lily Gunton to a Roman Prince arises when, in accordance with
his native custom, he asks her to write to his mother before the old
Princess herself has made any overtures. Lily refuses, the old
Princess stands pat, and Lily, having in the meantime inherited
"an extraordinary number of dollars," marries somebody else before
the Roman matron succumbs, too late, to that superior argument.
On the surface, then, this is a story of a war of pride in which the
pure waters of the Hudson have it all over the muddy floods of the
Tiber. Needless to say, the James of 1900 does not stop here.
Instead he lays irony over irony. Really being after Lily's fortune,
the Prince nevertheless bases his calculations all on love and is therefore in for a double loss—of the money as well as of the flattering
illusion that he has been loved for his own person. For like himself,
Lily has been in love merely with an external attribute, the glamor
of his name and of his past.

Yet even this is not the central focus. The story ends on a question: If Lily's Americanism is what made her subject to the appeal
of the Prince's "position," why should this same Americanism make
her hold out against the old Princess? What is the nature of this
Americanism? Is it—and we seem to see shades of Cooper—a
supreme sense of what aristocracy means, or is it the lack of all such
sense? These are questions which understandably agitate the Prince
and with which he confronts the Englishwoman through whose eyes
the reader in fact sees the whole episode. But she does not know

the answer: "With Americans one's lost," she says, for while they "think they have all sorts of things," all they really have is their Americanism, and "if you marry anything you marry that." Her outburst to the Prince suggests that the conflict of manners has not much abated since Bessie Alden and Lord Lambeth became its victims: "Why on earth don't you, all of you, leave them alone?" "They're an interest. But they're a nuisance. It's a question, very certainly, if they're worth the trouble they give."

The exclusive concern with manners is what makes "Miss Gunton of Poughkeepsie" a flicker of the *old* international flame. What gives it the color of the later period is the emphasis on the puzzle of Americanism. For more and more James's concern with Europe became a function of his preoccupation with the American character. Appearances to the contrary notwithstanding, he spoke prophetically when even in 1878 he said, "I know what I am about, and I have always my eyes on my native land."[28] "With Europe so constantly in requisition as the more salient American stage," as he put it thirty years later, the study of Americans might be as fruitful in Europe as at home. But while "An International Episode" gave almost equal emphasis to the American and European roles, the shift to James's more pronounced concern with its American aspects soon showed itself in the frequency with which Europeanized Americans replaced Europeans in his international drama. This happened particularly when the scene was not England but another European country, since James's reason for the shift was, in the first place, quite simply the kind of doubt expressed in *Portraits of Places,* the doubt of his ability to render foreign characters with anything but worthless approximation. In deciding upon the scene of *The Reverberator,* for instance, he took a vow never again to content himself with the *"à peu près* effects" of *The American.* Yet, since for sufficient reasons *The Reverberator* had to be laid in Paris, he found his solution, as he comments in the *Notebooks,* "where, with the help of Heaven, I hope to find many others in work to come, viz., in the idea of the Europeanized American," and this not simply as "an easier way" but because it promised "greater reality."[29]

If the English character did not seem to pose the problems of the French, the reason was the fundamental affinity which, as an American, James came to feel to it. This affinity, as we shall see, was central in what led to his expatriation. But that complex question, in order to be seen clearly, must be seen against the vividly colored background of his work. For his treatment of the international situation was integral with his personal problem as an American artist, was autobiographical in the sense in which all great fiction is autobiographical. This explains too why the young American girl became the dominant symbol in his international fiction. The content of that symbol, at any rate, serves almost as a master key to the unfolding of his vision.

 *The American as a Young Lady*

HOWELLS called James "the inventor" of the "international American girl," and indeed, with only a few exceptions, the protagonists in James's stories of the American experience of Europe are young girls, self-reliant, independent, American.[1] Thus the heroine of "Travelling Companions" (1870), his earliest "international" story, already anticipates Daisy Miller. And in "The Last of the Valerii" (1874) the contrast between the American heroine and her Italian husband, even in some of its phraseology, points forward all the way to *The Golden Bowl* of 1904: "The Conte Valerio's grandeur was doubtless nothing for a young American girl who had the air and almost the habits of a princess, to sound her trumpet about; but she was desperately in love with him, and not only her heart, but her imagination was touched." The largess of a princess and the active imagination are the qualities which more and more came to distinguish James's "international American girl," and the one who marries the Conte Valerio has them both.

There were several reasons for James's partiality, among them doubtless the impression made on him by his cousin Minny Temple.

Deeply affected by her death at the age of twenty-five, he wrote in 1870: "The more I think of her the more perfectly satisfied I am to have her translated from this changing realm of fact to the steady realm of thought. There she may bloom into a beauty more radiant than our dull eyes avail to contemplate." He had a presentiment that "her image" would "preside" in his "intellect." And the qualities he saw in her are indeed the ones which basically animate all of his American heroines: she was "a divinely restless spirit"; she incorporated for him the "moral spontaneity" which, he felt, distinguished American women from English. She was "an experiment of nature" and "a plant of pure American growth." She was, in short, the feminine counterpart of nature's nobleman or, in the words of his later formula, of the "heir of all the ages."[2]

But there were other, less personal, reasons why James represented America so consistently by its young women. His addiction to treating international social conflict in terms of marriage, in the first place, quite simply reflected a historical fact. In the years following the Civil War, intermarriage became an increasingly prominent, even notorious, feature of the social relations between America and Europe. And for reasons suggested by Mark Twain's repeated outbreaks against American "cringing" before nobility, against Newport, Rhode Island, as a "stud farm" of aristocracy, an "auction mart where the English nobilities come to trade hereditary titles for American girls and cash," the international marriage was almost invariably a marriage of the American woman to the European man.[3] It took this form so commonly, in fact, that when James wrote "Lady Barbarina," his one story of a marriage which goes the other way, he felt he had "to forge the very documents" of the case. As a rule, he stuck to the situation supplied by life.

Moreover, there were the limitations of James's upbringing by a father who feared that preparation for a career might narrow the minds of his boys, and who felt that to be a good human being was career enough for any man. In speaking of some of his early international stories, James therefore had to confess that he lacked "the particular initiation" into American life which would have enabled him to deal with the figures surrounding the American girl, the various "male appendages," always "thinkable only as the American 'business-man,'" and the older women, the American mothers—types, both, characterized for him primarily by their "inveterate blankness of surface." He confessed that, in them, all he was prepared to deal with was the "negative" side—their state of bewilderment, their helplessness in the face of European life, *their* lack of preparation for any but the most superficial relation with Europe as with an amusing and expensive toy, which performed for a charge but to which, in consequence, one was in no need to feel any responsibility. Hence, since he meant to treat the positive side of the spectacle, too, his exclusive concern with the young American girl was simply a result of his partial disability—simply, as he put it, a matter of being "shut up to what was left." For in the American girl in Europe, the characteristic American "blank-ness" of surface often underwent "a sea-change"; the innocence which in her elders all too often seemed mere destitution of knowl-edge, in her turned into the grace of youth so that "negatives were converted and became in certain relations lively positives and values."[4]

Fundamentally James's American girl is merely the American variety of a type to which, quite independent of international con-trast, he liked to assign the role of the protagonist in the struggle which is central in his work, the struggle of the individual to pro-tect his integrity and freedom against violation by the world. Almost all his heroines are engaged in a more or less outright and usually admirable conflict with the established order in which they live, from such early stories as "At Isella" (1871), whose Italian heroine revolts against the law which imposes obedience to the husband, to so late a novel as *The Outcry* (1911), whose English heroine rebels against the barren pride of an aristocracy which seems to have outlived its reason for being. What distinguishes all these women is that "moral spontaneity" which Minny Temple had had to such a high degree and which, in the words of one of his letters, sets them all off from the surrounding "realm of the cut and dried." But since they are often "innocent," too, since they illustrate the unawareness of life which struck him as "the most general appearance" of his compatriots in Europe, the young American girl became his primary symbol of the positive aspects of the American character.

The problem of the dual nature of "innocence" glanced at in such remarks, as well as its counterpart, the dual nature of "knowlege," of course transcends international contrasts. But in James's rendering of international conflict, "innocence" is to be found invariably on the American, "knowledge" on the European side, and the gradual change of his interpretation and evaluation of innocence and knowledge becomes therefore a reliable measure of the values which he attributed to Europe and America. A corollary of this change is his shift from comedy of manners, as in "An International Episode" (1878-79), to moral tragedy, as in *The Wings of the Dove* (1902), though often James does not keep the genres clearly separated, though "Daisy Miller" is a comedy whose heroine dies and *The Portrait of a Lady* is tragic despite the fact that its heroine lives. What matters more than life or death is the grounds on which James arouses our sympathy for the American girl, the causes of her ordeal as well as the fortitude with which she meets it. They constitute her story and, since she is his central symbol of the positive qualities he saw in America, the story of his own relation to Europe and America.

In a whole group of stories written in the late 1870's and early 1880's, the ordeal of the American girl is due not, as in "Madame de Mauves," to some alien code of conduct, but to the provincialism of her compatriots. For "Daisy Miller" (1878), "An International Episode" (1878-79), "The Pension Beaurepas" (1879), "A Bundle of Letters" (1879), even to some extent *The Portrait of a Lady* (1880-81), and certainly "The Point of View" (1882)—all belong to the collection of social data with which James began to record the relations of the two continents. With the exception of

The Portrait of a Lady, all these stories are satiric and ironic portrayals of various shades of provincialism.

In the Rucks of "The Pension Beaurepas" and the Rays of "A Bundle of Letters," provincialism may take the comparatively harmless form of vulgar rapacity on the part of the womenfolk, who spend their European days in a round of raids on the fashionable shops while the men, bored with Europe, more or less good-naturedly look on from behind their New York *Herald* in the lobby of the American bank. The stores, Mr. Ruck keeps saying, "after all, for the ladies, that's the principal interest"—until news of his own bankruptcy for the first time in his life rouses him to put a manly foot down. The mysterious American businessman can come in for James's sympathy if his inoffensive blandness has enough of liberal amplitude, for there are other such touching portraits in his gallery of male innocents abroad. But when provincialism turns aggressive, turns into cultural or social snobbery—as it is the more likely to do the more it is narrow—the note of indulgence subsides. We have already met an early example of the cultural snob in Clement Searle of "A Passionate Pilgrim" (1871), whose search for "the best" that England has to offer ends ironically in the discovery of social injustice. In "The Pension Beaurepas" Mrs. Church, who serves as a foil to the Rucks, whom she looks down on as "vulgar Americans," also insists that what she cares for is only "the best," and in "Pandora" (1884) the self-made American heroine takes her elderly parents to Europe "to see the best things." "I kept them three hours on the Acropolis," she says. "I guess they won't forget that!"—all of which strikes her European interlocutor as a pilgrimage all the more "extraordinary" as it has left no perceptible traces on her touchingly primitive taste.

"The best" is part of the facile vocabulary by which provincials and snobs make known their awareness of what goes in the way of "culture" and social form. It is all harmless food for amusement unless, indeed, it is made to justify the sort of unkindness which puzzles Bessie Alden in her worldly sister, or worse, petty tyranny

which actually violates the freedom of the individual spirit. This is
the case of Mrs. Church, who all unselfishly but with an iron hand
has dragged her daughter, on what she sweetly calls her "devoted
little errand, seeking, seeing, heeding, only the best," from one end
of Europe to another. For twelve years, since her mother is not
only a cultural but also a social snob, Aurora Church has been
exposed to one set of dreary "frumps" after another for no better
reason than that "they were *de leur pays!*" And if James sympathizes
more with her than with Mr. Ruck, it is for two reasons: In the
first place, aside from being young and therefore more exposed,
she is the victim of forces more sinister than the mere vulgar rapacity
of Mr. Ruck's women; but above all, there is much more to be
victimized in her than in the "voided man of business," for in her
the characteristic American "blankness" has undergone the sea-
change into the "lively positives and values" typical of the American
girl.

The classic example of this ordeal of the American girl at the
hands of her Europeanized compatriots is of course the story of
"Daisy Miller" (1878), based on a difference between American
and European manners, between the freedom allowed American
girls and the strict rules of propriety imposed upon European
jeunes filles, but not centrally concerned with it. For Daisy's troubles
are not caused by Europeans; it is her compatriots of the hotel world
and the expatriate colonies who misunderstand and plague her, and
this for two reasons which James carefully separates. The majority
of them, the women who set the social tone, are motivated largely
by the convert's zeal to advertise his conversion: they ostracize her,
as we are told, "for the benefit of observant Europeans," in order
to prove their own proficiency in the rules of the social "system"
they have adopted, in order to leave no doubt that they are fully
aware how "monstrous" the American freedoms of Daisy's conduct
are. They are social snobs pure and simple. Mrs. Costello is typical,
in all but the fact that her perch on the social ladder not only in
Rome but, much more telling, in Washington and New York, was

built long ago and high. Her fondness of "the minutely hierarchical constitution" of society is consequently deep, her eye for the social value of others unerring. It tells her at a glance that Daisy and her mother are "the sort of Americans one does one's duty" by "not accepting." Daisy "has that charming look that they all have," those free American girls, but Mrs. Costello "can't think where they pick it up"; and Daisy "dresses in perfection," but Mrs. Costello "can't think where they get their taste." For Daisy is a young lady who treats her mamma's courier "like a gentleman," and therefore, charm or no charm, taste or no taste, the "widow with a fortune" cannot accept her: "I would if I could," she says magnanimously, "but I can't."

So much for snobbery. But Winterbourne, the young American through whose eyes the reader largely sees Daisy, is no snob. His relation to her is determined by the question what her freedoms represent, whether she is "innocent" or not. And he misjudges her because he has lived abroad so long that "his instinct for such a question" is muddled, and his "reason" can only mislead him. So that his failure of judgment, too, is the result of a peculiarly American entanglement in the conflict of manners, a fact which becomes suddenly clear in the ironic end of the story. Giovanelli, the shabby Italian fortune hunter whose freely accepted attentions are what most compromises Daisy in the eyes of the American matrons and finally even of Winterbourne, ironically turns out to be the only one capable of recognizing and appreciating her innocence, and this in spite of the fact that it wears a color which in the women of his own country signifies something quite different. If this is linked with the suggestion that Daisy's innocence reveals to Giovanelli moral possibilities unknown in "the cynical streets of Rome," interesting as the implication may be as a foreshadowing of the later theme of *The Golden Bowl*, it has no part in James's central concern here. For in "Daisy Miller" his subject is not the possible contrast between American and Italian manners, although that provides the fuel for the dramatic conflict. His theme is what in the

Notebooks he described as "the eternal question of American snobbishness abroad,"[5] and the moral issue inherent in it is the death of individual responsibility at the hands of convention.

To say this, however, is to be more solemn than the story warrants. For it is a comedy, and this not only because it portrays the enemy of the spirit much more sharply than the spirit itself. Daisy has after all something of the foolish about her in addition to what she has of the brave. And when Howells said that "while her youth lasts she is an angelic, a divine fool, with caprices that have the quality of inspirations,"[6] he gave her credit for something which some of her sisters among James's freely adventuring American maidens may demonstrate, but which in her we have to take very much for granted. Daisy's virtues are courage and a stubbornness which amounts to endurance, and it may be only fair to assume that they are nourished by some bright inner flame; but James does not tell us what that flame feeds on, what the source of Daisy's power of resistance is. The simple fact is that "Daisy Miller" is first of all a document of social relations, like "Pandora" or "The Siege of London," comedies whose American heroines also raise the question of innocence because their conduct, like Daisy's, is seen through the puzzled consciousness of a member of the world of convention. Significantly, it is in connection with those stories that James mentions her in the *Notebooks,* not in connection with, say, *The Portrait of a Lady,* despite the fact that Isabel Archer, its heroine, belongs to the same independent, protestant, nonconformist sisterhood. James's characterization of Isabel, in his preface to her story, as "an intelligent but presumptuous girl" affronting her destiny,[7] might well be applied to Daisy, but the difference between the two stories is that Isabel's is seen from within; hence—since it, too, is the story of an ordeal—the tragic tone, which Daisy's story, despite her death, entirely lacks.

While "Daisy Miller" grew from the author's sense of a social situation, of a set of relations, a sense which led more or less naturally to comedy of manners, the germ of *The Portrait of a*

Lady was wholly in his sense of the heroine's character. And the specific problem—since, as he said, "millions of presumptuous girls, intelligent or not intelligent, daily affront their destiny"— was how to make her story interesting. James's solution was logical and typical: it was to "place the centre of the subject in the young woman's own consciousness"; it was to focus constantly on the question, "what will she *do?*" It was quite simply to *make* her character interesting. The type was there; you met the free American girl in Europe wherever you looked; her charm was "inextinguish- able." Daisy Miller demonstrated it, Bessie Alden did, Aurora Church tried to account for it when she protested that an American girl was not a *jeune fille* but "an intelligent responsible creature." Others were to demonstrate it; and some few exceptions, like Miss Ruck of "The Pension Beaurepas" and later Selina Wing of "A London Life" (1888), by demonstrating the possible limitations of the type and the dangers to which it was exposed when the charm had to subsist on "a very light substance,"[8] largely served to prove the rule. But to make the charm of the American girl do for inter- est, one had to "translate her into the highest terms" of her formula "and as nearly as possible moreover into *all* of them." This, the core of the preface to *The Portrait of a Lady,* is James's account of the origins of Isabel Archer, and explains why it is that we have to go to her portrait in order to understand the nature of the "inspirations" which Howells believed to be animating Daisy Miller's caprices.

The Portrait of a Lady, however, is not alone a summation of what James had come to see as the positive qualities which contact and conflict with Europe could bring out in the American character. Incorporated in its texture and thereby contributing to the projec- tion of the heroine's experience are many of the conventional elements which were part of the history of that contact. Above all, there is Henrietta Stackpole, the American lady reporter whom James uses as a means to dramatize, ironically but sympathetically nevertheless, certain phases of the American tradition of democratic criticism of Europe. It has long been her desire to come to Europe to report to her countrymen in a series of letters "from the radical point of view," an enterprise, as James tells us, "the less difficult as she knew perfectly in advance what her opinions would be and to how many objections most European institutions lay open." She is aggressively suspicious of all that smacks of privilege and class, and most of all of American prostration before European standards. But she finds, poor Henrietta, that her most popular letters are those from romantic Spain, one of which in particular, dated from Irving's Alhambra and entitled "Moors and Moonlight," passes for her masterpiece. Henrietta's career serves mainly as a kind of comic counterpoint to Isabel's melancholy story, since she ends not only by tolerating all that she at first suspects, but by marrying a thorough Britisher and, unlike Isabel, finding happiness in her marriage.

Isabel too, however, is for all her pride of independence entangled in conventional American ways of thinking. When she first comes to Europe, she checks everything she sees against the "descriptions in the books." She asks a great many questions without listening very carefully to the answers or at most sticking them away in her bag of information for later consideration according to her own good judgment. When told, for instance, that in England young girls do not sit with gentlemen alone late at night, though admitting that she is very fond of her own Albany ways, she says, "I always want to know the things one shouldn't do." "So as to do them?" her monitor asks. No, she says, "so as to choose"—and immediately she is alive to us in all her innocent self-assurance. With a good deal of light irony at first, James evokes the portrait of a girl who, although her thoughts are a "tangle of vague outlines" of delusions and errors which have never been "corrected by the judgement of people speaking with authority," is animated by a generous portion of self-esteem. With her "meagre knowledge, her inflated ideals, her confidence at once innocent and dogmatic," she has some of Euphemia de Mauves's romantic exaltation as well as some of Daisy Miller's presumptuous unconcern for the conventions of the society in which she moves; she more or less combines the various terms of the formula of the American girl.

But she is also an interpretation of the type in "the highest terms" of that formula, and what distinguishes her from those others is the high degree to which she possesses the primary colors of James's moral spectrum: integrity, intelligence, imagination, all of which contribute—and this is the source of the tragic tone of her story—not only to her strength but equally to her weakness. Knowing nothing of how a man escapes whipping, she hopes, for instance, that all she need demand of her fellow-men is that they treat her after her desert; and she reaches what is probably the height of her naïve presumption when she affirms as much to the man whose discreet generosity has, unknown to her, just made her rich and thereby free to follow her "determination to see, to try, to know" the world. This same hope is part of another and hardly more humble one, the "infinite hope that she should never do anything wrong." But what seems mere presumption and what is of course part of her inexperienced youth turns into the positive value of a rigorous conscience when the chance of injuring another person, even if presented as a mere contingency, causes her to hold her breath in anxiety, when the discovery of "her mere errors of feeling" can make her tremble "as if she had escaped from a trap which might have caught her and smothered her." And it is the combination of this moral sensitivity, often so close to the absurd, with "a certain nobleness of imagination which," as James says, "rendered her a good many services and played her a good many tricks" which makes her appealing in all her ludicrousness and which, above all, arouses in the observer a sense of high expectation.

Expectation is, in fact, the structural principle on which *The Portrait of a Lady* is built. In order to make the question "What will she do?" significant, James frees Isabel from all external inhibitions. He makes her an orphan so that Mrs. Touchett, her aunt, may bring her to England. Next, her cousin Ralph Touchett, intrigued by her personality, causes his father to change his will in such a manner as to make her rich. Ralph wants "to put money in her purse" so that she may be able to meet the requirements of her imagination freely. And after his father's death, we watch with him what she makes of her freedom. What she does make of it, what in the end Ralph calls "a generous mistake," is to marry Gilbert Osmond, an American expatriate living in Florence, not exactly a fortune hunter, but a subtle kind of snob, whose aesthetic refinement hides a complete emptiness of the spirit—whose whole life, in fact, is a hollow structure of calculated effects. "The idea of the whole thing," James said in one of his preliminary notes, "is that the poor girl, who has dreamed of freedom and nobleness, who has done, as she believes, a generous, natural, clear-sighted thing, finds herself in reality *ground in the very mill of the conventional*";[9] and the last phrase, here italicized, is the final judgment which in the novel James puts into Ralph's mouth, too.

Ralph is not to be identified with James. He dramatizes merely James's expectant sympathy with the American quality which Isabel represents—the imagination, as he keeps calling it, which is really a kind of spiritual energy. Henrietta Stackpole, on the other hand, dramatizes James's awareness of the vulnerability of this imagination when, as in Isabel's case, it lacks the authoritative discipline of experience. And the question posed by the conflict between these two attitudes is the question which Isabel's story answers. At the moment when the world is all before her, Ralph is alive to the possibilities which his generosity has put within her reach; Henrietta, at the same moment, skeptical and earthbound, is alive to the dangers it exposes her to, moral dangers which she sees lurking in Isabel's addiction to living, as she says, in the world of her own dreams. It is the very tendency Isabel is proud of: success, she says, is "to see some dream of one's youth come true," and the definition, imaginative as it may be, contains the very dangers Henrietta fears. For what Isabel in her young egotism lacks is the experience which teaches that men are bound to make mistakes, that no man is entire in himself, that "dreams" can be the very pride that comes before the fall. Like Daisy Miller, she is a kind of capricious fool. What distinguishes her caprices from Daisy's is that James shows us clearly what animates them.

This indicates the shift of James's focus. In the earlier story the picture he gives is all of manners, all in terms of Daisy's relation with society; in *The Portrait* it is largely of the heroine's relation with herself, so that her story is a story of moral clarification. Though from the first Isabel is intent on doing right, her intention is perverted by her egotism, which prevents her from realizing the dangers to which inexperience exposes her. She believes not only in the freedom of her own will but also in the sufficiency of her own mind as a guide, and her story—forecast in Henrietta's early warning to her that in the long run one cannot "escape disagreeable duties by taking romantic views," that one must be prepared "on many occasions in life to please no one at all," not even oneself— is a denial of both. What remains with Isabel to the end is the determination to do what is right. "As seems right," Ralph Touchett says to her at the end, "you think a great deal about that," and the simplicity of Isabel's "Of course one must," spoken after she has learned to a sufficiency how prophetic Henrietta's warning was, gives the measure of her moral integrity. This is no more the easy hope of an imagination "by habit ridiculously active," but the lesson drawn conscientiously from the discipline of misery.

The general pattern of Isabel's story is the pattern underlying many of James's stories of the American girl in Europe. Their common theme is nothing more than a variation on the theme of the lived life, probably the most constant concern of his work. The full life—almost axiomatically the good life—is of course not mere activity, but consists of experience had and understood, experience appropriated to oneself and made into knowledge. Experience missed—rejected by oneself or withheld by others—and experience misunderstood, perverted, is what is bad. What is therefore necessary for the full and good life are the opportunity and the freedom which provide experience; the desire, the energy, the curiosity which takes it; and the intelligence which understands it. If these are given, then living consists of moving from unawareness to awareness, the highest good in which intellect, beauty, and morality merge in a conscience that is conscious or in a consciousness that is good. Inevitably, in James, the fine consciousness and the fine conscience are in the end identical, merge in "lucidity."

The quality which the American girl invariably has is the eager curiosity, the freedom of the mind, and her story consists either of the struggle against the limitations on her freedom imposed from without, or—if the freedom is granted—of the growth of her awareness. In the first case her antagonists, the representatives of some sort of convention, attempt to restrain her, and the result is comedy of manners whose social satire is aimed at them—that is, at people like the American matrons in "Daisy Miller," like Mrs. Westgate and Percy Beaumont of "An International Episode," or Mrs. Church of "The Pension Beaurepas." In the second case, when her story is the story of her growing awareness, the emphasis may be either on her initial ignorance or on her capacity for learning. If it is the first, her story is a story of disenchantment like the stories of Euphemia de Mauves and Bessie Alden, who find out the "truth" about aristocracy, an institution based on a false criterion of human worth, a formalization of life which violates nature by asserting superiority on grounds which do not insure superiority.

This, too, is frequently the emphasis of James's early stories, comedies whose irony is directed largely at the illusions of the heroines; illusions which, because they are founded on books, on "fictions," are a sign of their ignorance of "life" and, where Europe is concerned, are typically American. To some extent this is true of the early parts of *The Portrait of a Lady,* but the total emphasis of this novel is on Isabel's capacity for learning. Isabel, too, finds out the "truth" about a kind of pretended superiority, finds out the empty vulgarity hidden under Osmond's pretense of intellectual and cultural refinement. Above all, however, she finds out the truth about herself: that she is uninformed and therefore, in spite of her intelligence and good will, incapable of good judgment, and that the experience of her friends, particularly of Ralph Touchett, constitutes a valid authority.

This emphasis on Isabel's inner growth indicates a double transition in James's treatment of the American girl. For one thing, she now becomes his central concern; his focus shifts from Europe as the object of the American imagination to this imagination itself, and from the blankness or the illusion which is due to the lack of experience to the knowledge which is the result of experience; from the elimination of the mistaken notions about Europe, the object, to the acquisition of substance on the part of the American girl, the subject. In a word, it shifts from her lack of experience to her getting experience, and from her passively being to her actively doing, which—and this is the second aspect of the transition—is always proof of her curiosity and moral vitality. So that the transition is also from her actual weakness to her potential strength. In this *The Portrait of a Lady* stands midway between James's earlier stories and the great novels of his maturity, which focus primarily on the fulfilment of the promise contained in the energy, the appetite for life, "the lively positives and values" which in the American girl are hidden under the characteristic American "blankness."

As James's focus shifts from outward to inward, from manners to morals, the American girl becomes the symbol of American strength, and finally the "heiress of all the ages," whose virtue is tried and tested and tempered by exposure to the world, and who, like Maggie Verver of *The Golden Bowl,* inherits the earth. Maggie, Milly Theale of *The Wings of the Dove,* and finally Rosanna Gaw of *The Ivory Tower,* thoroughly fulfil the high expectations which Isabel arouses. In them, the "idealization" of a "real superiority," of which F. R. Leavis speaks in connection with Isabel,[10] is complete because what is in Isabel a kind of tragic flaw in them has been purged by the discipline of experience. Even *The Wings of the Dove,* in spite of the death of its heroine, is in a sense less deeply tragic than *The Portrait of a Lady* because the defeat of the heroine, as far as it is a defeat at all, is due to the enemy without and to a failure of the body but not of the spirit. It is a story of redemption, in that sense a "divine comedy," where Isabel's story is the story of a fall, and therefore tragic. Or, viewing *The Portrait of a Lady* as a development from the earlier stories, we see that their comic irony is transformed into tragic irony simply because James has shifted the emphasis from cloistered innocence, which lacks the strength to deal with the world, to the strength which comes from experience and exposure.

This is what distinguishes Isabel's determination from Bessie Alden's gentle firmness. Bessie does not undergo the test of real suffering; Isabel does, and the solid substance of the tragic figure reveals itself primarily in her ability to suffer without being thereby corrupted, in the fact that she transforms her suffering into a clearer knowledge of her moral needs. This is emphasized in the conclusion of the novel, when Caspar Goodwood offers to help her "save" what is left of her life. What he offers her is freedom from responsibility—"Trust me as if I had the care of you," he says. It is an offer which has never tempted her, but her last refusal of him shows that what she has always wanted, even in the early days of her innocent presumption, was the freedom not from but of responsibility. All she now knows is that there is "a very straight path" for her, and her return to Rome—so strikingly similar to Hester Prynne's final return to her New England cottage—is not so much into Osmond's prison as into the freedom of her duty.

To say this is to interpret the Isabel of the beginning of the novel in the light of the Isabel of the end, almost to credit a sister of Daisy Miller with the virtue of a Milly Theale. For in *The Portrait of a Lady* we seem indeed to catch James in the very act of idealizing the American girl. This impression and the direction of his thought which it indicates are borne out by his revisions for the New York Edition.[11] They emphasize Isabel's links with both his earlier and his later American heroines—the romantic approach to life which Henrietta Stackpole fears as her danger and the free imagination which Ralph Touchett admires as her strength. But, as Matthiessen points out, the early description of Isabel in Chapter VI was left unchanged, including the crucial sentence—"She would be an easy victim of scientific criticism if she were not intended to awaken on the reader's part an impulse more tender and more purely expectant"—which seems to arrest the very moment when James turns from comic to tragic irony. For what allows her story to be tragic is precisely this dual aspect of her character, the fact that the moral self-reliance which makes her admirable also makes her vulnerable, so that her destiny, in the best tragic manner due to the particular conjunction of character and circumstance, moves us by illustrating the waste of good.

Isabel's uninformed vitality is in sharp contrast with the studied formality of Osmond. Meeting him when her senses are charmed and her fancy stirred by her first experience of Italy, she is touched by "an indefinable beauty" in what seems to be his quiet devotion to private values. Her sense that he is "helpless and ineffectual" arouses in her a maternal tenderness and a desire to act with her "charged hands" as his good "providence." Very much like Ralph Touchett, when he puts money in *her* purse, she anticipates in her marriage to Osmond an "infinite vista of multiplied life"—a vista which before long she finds, however, turned into a "dark, narrow alley with a dead wall at the end." For everything in Osmond is pose; "his culture, his cleverness, his amenity"—all hide an appalling egotism. His contempt for the world turns out to be the shabbiest kind of snobbery. His deeply calculated effects, though produced by no vulgar means, have after all the vulgarest of motives. He is in sum the very antithesis of herself. Under his touch, she comes to feel, everything withers, under his look everything spoils; his very presence is a blight. Her way of looking at life, the very fact of her "having a mind of her own at all," is a personal offense to him, and he comes to hate her with the deepseated antagonism of death for life. For, worse than a mere snob, he is the incarnate negation of the living spirit and, in his efforts to cut Isabel down to his own measure, guilty—like Hawthorne's Ethan Brand and Chillingworth—of the "unpardonable sin" of tampering with "the sanctity of the human heart." More and more, as Isabel's eyes open to all this, the sinister note increases and throws the shadow of a deep corruption over all that has seemed exquisite.

It is important to remember that Osmond is not a European but an American expatriate. James emphasizes this in a significant passage, put in the mouth of Madame Merle, his accomplice and herself one of the "wretched set." She speaks with the cold lucidity which comes from experience. "If we're not good Americans we're certainly poor Europeans," she tells Isabel. They have no "natural place" in Europe, no roots in the soil; at best they are collectors, devoting themselves, as Madame Merle herself does, to "some rather good old damask," or measuring their lives, as Osmond does, by the purchase of "an old silver crucifix at a bargain"—activities which are a special form of the failing peculiar to Americans in Europe, the taking of the form for the thing, illustrated already in the social snobbery of the American matrons in "Daisy Miller" or the cultural snobbery of Mrs. Church in "The Pension Beaurepas." It is also the cause of Isabel's initial failure to see the utter emptiness hidden under Osmond's superficial refinement. In Osmond it takes the form of a cultivation of tradition so perverted that he tells Isabel, if one does not have one, "one must immediately proceed to make it." And indeed she finds that he has "a very large collection" of traditions though from what source derived she cannot learn. Philip Rahv has pointed out the significance of Osmond as "a cultural type," as a portrait of the American intellectual, in whom a "residue of 'colonial' feeling" betrays itself by a tendency "to take literally" what his European counterpart is "likely to take metaphorically and imaginatively." It is all the more surprising that Rahv can speak of Osmond as "virtually a European,"[12] which indeed he is not.

For James is careful to distinguish between the American and the European antagonists of the American girl—from "Daisy Miller" to *The Golden Bowl*, where the distinction is a central part of his theme. In *The Portrait of a Lady* it is dramatized in the mutual antipathy of Osmond and Lord Warburton. Though the traditionalism of both represents a threat to the freedom of Isabel's spirit, their relations to tradition differ fundamentally. Osmond is deeply corrupt, deeply false. His traditionalism is "altogether a thing of forms, a conscious, calculated attitude," designed to cover his lack of individual substance. His seclusion on his hilltop in a villa filled with bibelots but empty of people is a symbol of his expatriation not merely from America but from all human community, from which traditions spring and which, above all, they serve. His perversion is underlined by the fact that his traditions not only take no account of such fundamental moral values as simple "decency" but actually include things so "hideously unclean" as to make Isabel feel like pushing "back her skirts." All this adds up to a sinister villainy which the picture of Lord Warburton wholly lacks. Warburton is not false simply because he is not rootless. The traditions which the other pretends to, he possesses securely, legitimately—which is the reason why Osmond desires him so immensely as a husband for his daughter. For her illegitimacy and his attempt to force her into the marriage with the nobleman are more than a convenience of plot; they are both symbolic of Osmond's relation to human society.

Yet, Osmond's corruption is of course not the result of his being an American. What it illustrates is the danger which Europe exposes Americans to. It is a danger inherent in the very process of ordering experience significantly—the danger that the order, the form, which results from the action of the spirit on experience, becomes frozen and self-sufficient and finally imprisons the very spirit which gave it birth. It is the danger typical of Europe, where the past lingers not only in the form of ruins and associations but in the form also of institutions which tend to perpetuate themselves even when their reason for being if not their meaning is antiquated. Emerson's rejection of the authority of books or of the single Revelation are examples of the American criticism of such frozen forms in the fields of philosophy and religion. The contrast between natural and artificial aristocracy is an example of it in the field of social and political thought which James, as we have seen, used in some of his earliest tales and of which a trace lingers in Isabel's relation to Lord Warburton.

Her reasons for refusing the Englishman's proposal indeed go to the very center of James's vision of international contrast. It is not that she objects to the "aristocratic life"; it is rather that her notions of it differ from Warburton's. She thinks of it as "simply the union of great knowledge with great liberty," and it is for her liberty that she fears. Not that Warburton would imprison her as Osmond tries to do. There is no doubt of his consideration, his kindness; there is nothing in the least sinister about him. Yet she regards his proposal somehow as the design of "a territorial, a political, a social magnate" to draw her into a "system," the system of which his sisters are such charming but such ominously pale products.

Lord Warburton's misfortune is that his eminence lies in a "collection of attributes and powers" independent of his individual character, no matter how appealing *that* may be. In social and political terms he is a nobleman of birth; in James's psychological terms he is the expensive product of cultivation and therefore demands consideration which Isabel does not have the patience to give. She is used to judging people on the basis of "character and wit," on the basis of the question whether they please "her sublime soul"—according to rules too simple to serve as a measure of Warburton's qualifications. In a word, marriage to him fails "to support any enlightened prejudice in favour of the free exploration of life"; there is "something stiff and stupid" in the system which has made him—all of which is borne in upon her with emphatic energy by a letter from Caspar Goodwood burning in her pocket at the very time Warburton makes his plea. Goodwood, though he too threatens her liberty, represents a power which is in no degree a matter of his "advantages" but entirely a matter of the spirit which sits "in his clear-burning eyes like some tireless watcher at a window." And the memory of *that* power is fatal to Warburton's hopes.

The American manufacturer, engineer, mover of men, and the English Lord represent qualities which James considered more and more as typical of America and Europe. But it is important to see that they represent these qualities in a neutral equilibrium of positive and negative, that each satisfies where the other does not, that if in Warburton the man is smothered by the "system," Goodwood shows his appetites "too simply and artlessly"; that if Warburton's virtues are too much cultivated, Goodwood's are not cultivated enough. For American vitality and European discipline both had alike their potentials for good and evil. Nor does James's international fiction rest, as some critics have asserted, on a distinction between moral and aesthetic values, between "cultural" inferiority but "moral" superiority in America and their opposites in Europe.[13] In fact, wherever such explanations are attempted, the simplification leads to more or less flagrant distortions and misreadings of the moral significance of individual characters. Art and life are in James's view of things much too closely related, "the house of life and the palace of art," as he recalls in *A Small Boy and Others,* became at an early time too "mixed and interchangeable"[14] to allow so simple an opposition between moral and aesthetic values.

How close their relation was for him a story like "The Figure in the Carpet" makes clear: "Literature was a game of skill, and skill meant courage, and courage meant honour, and honour meant passion, meant life." Even more forthright, certainly more personal, is a letter to H. G. Wells: "It is art that *makes* life," James wrote, "and I know of no substitute whatever for the force and beauty of its process." Wells answered that he could "read sense into" this statement only by assuming that James was using *art* "for every

conscious human activity." "I use the word," Wells added, "for a
research and attainment that is technical and special"—and nothing
could have formed a clearer contrast with the intimate relation
James saw between art and life, and with the organic relation of
form and content which derives from it. Consciousness is, ultimately,
the soul of James's art, in which "force and beauty," the moral and
the aesthetic, become one. For him, "the 'moral' sense of a work
of art," as he said in the preface to *The Portrait of a Lady,* depended
directly on "the amount of felt life concerned in producing it." And
in the preface to "The Lesson of the Master," which is perhaps his
most extended single discourse on the subject, he defined the work
of the artist, the "intelligent painter of life," as the midwife assist-
ance he gives at the birth of "true meanings."[15] Stephen Dedalus
went forth to encounter "the reality of experience" and in the
smithy of his soul to forge "the uncreated conscience" of his race.
It is what James, too—hesitantly and without the megalomania—
again and again set out to do.

His view of the process of art, moreover, was closely paralleled
by his view of the process of history, both being integral to his
view of life. If the virtue of art was to create "true meanings,"
historical experience, too, made for order, for form—for the manners, conventions, traditions governing society. These results of the
continuity of European experience, of European history "as a still-
felt past,"[16] therefore, are in James's view by no means necessarily
inimical to life. They need not smother the spirit; they may liberate
it. This, in *The Portrait of a Lady,* is the meaning of the contrast
between Osmond, who attempts to stifle Isabel's freedom, and Ralph
Touchett, also a "Europeanized American," who provides her with
freedom in order to see the promise of her spirit fulfilled. And the
dual nature of convention is made explicit in the crucial chapter
(XLII) in which Isabel analyzes the mistake she has made in marrying Osmond: "He had told her he loved the conventional," and it
had seemed to her "a noble declaration" of his love of "harmony and
order and decency and of all the stately offices of life." But with

"incredulous terror," as time passes, Isabel discovers that the house of Osmond's thought is a house of darkness and suffocation to which his "beautiful mind" gives neither light nor air, a prison of the spirit or its tomb, instead of, as she thought, a noble mansion which it has built and in which it lives. For Osmond has divorced convention and tradition from life.

He and, to a minor extent, Lord Warburton, then, represent the danger inherent in the European emphasis on order. But a similar danger inheres also in the America which James contrasted with this Europe. The ultimate good in James's view of things, as we have seen, is the awareness which results from the full life, the kind of awareness which is central in the art which *"makes* life, makes interest, makes importance." And while James's images of America are rarely without the vital energy which constitutes the needed impulse for living fully, yet this energy—like the European sense of form—has potentialities for harm as well as for profit. Its promise may be broken. It, too, may turn tyrannical; it, too, may corrupt if, refusing to submit to the creative discipline of the spirit, it explodes in sheer mindless activity. This, as we shall see, is implicit in a number of stories reflecting James's reaction to his renewed acquaintance with America in 1904, a reaction which led him to a surprising re-evaluation even of the type of the American girl. But long before this, he had occasionally touched upon the negative aspects of the free American energy.

It is a striking fact that while the promise of unencumbered American vitality is in James almost invariably symbolized by the young American girl, the questions which it raises and the threats which it contains are usually dramatized in American men. An exception to this rule is Christopher Newman of *The American*.[17] But he is a conscious creation of one of nature's noblemen, and the traditional contrast between natural and artificial aristocracy in James soon transcended the limits of social and political criticism and merged with his distinction between "character" as a gift of nature and "culture" as an accumulation of social experience—a distinction which seems to have derived from observation and which entered into some of his earliest tales. Thus "Travelling Companions" (1870) contains an "excellent representative American" who points forward directly to Newman: "Without taste, without culture or polish, he nevertheless produced an impression of substance in character, keenness in perception, and intensity in will, which effectually redeemed him from vulgarity." And the narrator, a young American brought up largely in Europe, echoes traditional American language when he adds that the combination of these qualities with tolerance, self-confidence, fearlessness "might have been very fairly termed aristocratic." Yet in part, the terms are literally those of one of James's letters from England of the year before "Travelling Companions" was published: "We seem a people of *character*," he had written to his mother, "we seem to have energy, capacity and intellectual stuff in ample measure," but all "with *culture* quite left out. It's the absolute and incredible lack of *culture* that strikes you in common travelling Americans."[18]

The contrast between "character" and "culture," related also to the distinction between "imagination" and "observation" which "Travelling Companions" and *Roderick Hudson* make in connection with the criticism of art, is part of the whole question of the values of innocence and experience in human life. But after *The American* James relegated his male Americans more and more to negative roles. Christopher Newman dwindles into the tired businessman, lost in Europe and leaving exploration to his women—into a Mr. Ruck or a Mr. Dosson, men who still have a certain loose liberality about them, still some of the "good-humored tolerance" of the representative American, but not his energy or his keenness. Or Newman loses his poise and large dignity and turns into a figure of rash aggressive energy which threatens, as Goodwood does, the freedom necessary for the creative exploration of life. Or, worst of all, Goodwood loses the intelligence and the spirit which burn so clearly in his eyes and wastes his energy in ill-conceived activity. The imaginative and intelligent eagerness for life, at any rate, James more and more exclusively incorporates in the young American girl, who thereby comes to take the place of Nature's nobleman in the contrast between American idealism and European formality.[19]

Yet the question of "character" and "culture" persists in all this. The contrast between Caspar Goodwood and Lord Warburton, for instance, is repeated in "The Modern Warning" (1888), though with much less art, in the contrast between Macarthy Grice, another American man of affairs, and Sir Rufus Chasemore, both representing what is strong in their countries. The American, James tells us, is "thin, dry, fine," and his face suggests that there is "more in him of the spirit than of the letter"; he looks at the same time "unfinished" and "mature." The Englishman, on the other hand, has "more detail about him, something stippled and retouched, an air of having been more artfully fashioned, in conformity with traditions and models." The balanced contrast with which the passage begins trails off, however, into an irony directed mainly at the American's Anglophobia.

The subject of the story, as the *Notebooks* show, had been suggested to James by the publication of one of the violent English criticisms of America, a book of warning against the "horrors of democracy" addressed to the English themselves, and it is all the more remarkable therefore that James's critical focus, in spite of occasional references to "the misery and brutality of the British populace" and in spite of his portrayal of the Englishman's complacent conservatism, is largely on the prejudices and self-consciousness of American patriotism. For characteristically, James is barely concerned with the conflict of political principles. What interests him is the personal problem of the American girl caught in a conflict between opposed loyalties—to the English husband and to her country and the brother who represents it. The story begins as an ironic comedy: "One tells a girl one adores her and she replies that she doesn't care so long as one doesn't adore her compatriots"—the exasperated outcry of the British suitor is representative. But a large number of the traditional elements of the Anglo-

American conflict of manners—the repugnance of the American male for the almost epidemic Anglo-American marriage, his fear of English snubs, his highly rhetorical scorn of aristocracy, to mention a few—are insufficiently dramatized, and the fundamental weakness of the story is emphasized by a tragic ending wholly unprepared for.

Another story of the same year and a real comedy is much more dramatically successful. *The Reverberator* (1888) has obvious parallels with *The American:* the central issue is again the marriage of a simple American to a member of high French society. But in the twelve years since the publication of *The American* James had come to feel that his treatment of the French in that novel lacked accuracy. Hence his decision to substitute for French nobility a family of Catholic Carolinian *émigrés,* the Proberts, who have come to Paris in the time of Louis Philippe and are more royal than the king. They resemble Osmond in their exaggeration of an assumed mode of life, though—thanks to an origin less indistinct than his—their relation to the traditions they have adopted is less specious. Gaston Probert, the youngest of the family, falls in love with Francie Dosson but finds his family opposed to his marrying her, just as in *The American* the Bellegardes oppose the marriage of their daughter to Christopher Newman. James's focus and with it the motives he gives his characters differ, however, fundamentally from those in his earlier novel. While Claire de Cintré in the earlier novel is a simple victim of the powerful and criminal family will, while James pays little attention to her inner conflict, the question whether Gaston is going to assert his independence is now a central issue involving his individual moral existence. The family opposition, too, is much more convincingly motivated. The melodramatic wickedness of the Bellegardes is in the Proberts replaced by a powerful regard for tradition and a shrinking from what they consider Francie's vulgarity. This makes for the "greater reality" which James promised himself from his shift from French characters to the Europeanized Americans more familiar to him.

Whether the Proberts' objections to Francie are justified becomes a real question, for her conduct is highly ambiguous.

The complication arises from the element which originally suggested the story to James. In the *Notebooks* he records the incident of a "scribbling, publishing, indiscreet, newspaperized American girl" who enjoyed the hospitality of some members of the "conservative, still shockable" Venetian society, only to babble of her experiences afterward in an "inconceivable letter" to a New York newspaper. "One sketches one's age but imperfectly," James notes, if one does not touch upon "the invasion, the impudence and shamelessness, of the newspaper and the interviewer, the devouring *publicity* of life, the extinction of all sense between public and private."[20] In the story the journalist becomes George Flack, an old acquaintance of the Dossons, who publishes what Francie tells him of the family affairs of the Proberts in a sensational "society letter" to his paper (the *Reverberator* of the title). And the Proberts, not unreasonably blaming Francie for the outrage, now refuse to go through with the marriage. Gaston is at first too puzzled by Francie's motives to rebel against the family will, though at the last moment he asserts his independence and thereby saves his individual moral being.

As far as the story concerns him, it ends in the victory of self-reliance over the forces of rigid convention represented by the Proberts. In this view of the matter, Francie has acted as "the finger of providence" showing Gaston the way to "his freedom of spirit." But Francie's prodigious "innocence" makes the ways of providence mysterious indeed, for what puzzled James in the woman reporter of his original anecdote—that she *"should* have acted in good faith"[21]—still puzzles the reader in Francie's "inconceivabilities of ignorance." All she can say in answer to the Proberts' mortification is, "I had no idea you'd all feel so badly. I didn't mean any harm. I thought you'd like it." And all the Proberts can conclude is that *"c'est un sens qui lui manque,"* that she is incorrigibly vulgar. Indeed, while watching her babble to Flack even the reader is tempted to ask at times whether her unawareness is not dangerously close to stupidity. But she is not meant to be stupid. What makes her behave in the manner which strikes the Proberts as so indelicate is precisely a certain delicacy—the desire to make amends to Flack, whom she has refused to marry and who has brought her and Gaston together.

Moreover, she is incapable of conceiving what a scoundrel Flack is. For his abuse of her trust is not a mere matter of vulgar journalism. *He* is not without the sense of what his letter to the *Reverberator* means; he has written it just because he hopes that it may make Francie's marriage to Gaston impossible. But if he thereby illustrates the particular form of moral corruption to which American energy is exposed when no discipline has made it sensitive to social and moral needs, James is far from taking the side of the Proberts. His sympathies are entirely with the two young figures of Francie and Gaston, "so fresh, so candid, so meant for confidence," as he sees them, but by the lack of candor on the part of both the unscrupulous Flack and the suave Proberts forced into a "wan defiance" of each other. Very much like Bessie Alden and Lord Lambeth before them, Francie and Gaston are ground in a conflict of manners in which the artificiality of the Proberts is as a negative force second only to Flack's hypocrisy. Whatever sympathy James may have for them in their trial by yellow journalism is highly qualified. If it is for the discretion, the disciplined sense of decorum which Flack so entirely lacks, it is not for the irregularities it may hide. Whatever in their own conduct raises questions about the probity which even their name seems to advertise, far from having James's indulgence, serves merely to emphasize how spurious their moral position is. Though the melodramatic black and white of *The American* has here given way to a delicate balance of comic grays, the Proberts are with Flack clearly among the antagonists in the drama, not because they allow themselves certain carefully guarded liberties, but primarily because they try to withhold from Gaston a much more important "freedom of the spirit."

A French commentator has recently endorsed the reality of James's picture: "En France, dans les milieux aristocratiques, on tient la dignité et l'intégrité de la famille comme sacrées," and "si un conflict éclate entre cette puissante entité sociale et une déstinée individuelle, c'est le bonheur ou la personne de l'individu qui sont sacrifiés."[22] But our French critic, significantly, does not seem to have realized that this aspect of life in France "dans les milieux aristocratiques" is exactly what James meant to criticize, here as much earlier in *The American*. For believing that James sided with the Proberts quite generally, he sees *The Reverberator* as a milestone in James's education in "l'art de la vie élégante." It is a curiously revealing definition, this French definition of James's "education"—"au sens que son compatriote et contemporain, Henry Adams, a donné a ce terme, c'est-à-dire son initiation, à la française, à l'appréciation artistique des valeurs essentielles de la vie"[23]—for it wholly overlooks James's profound moral preoccupation. But the astigmatism of this French view becomes clearest in its conclusion that James came to see puritan America as "fermée à la spontanéité du coeur, aux delicatesses de l'esprit et à la joie de vivre." For while this may apply to the America represented by a Flack, it does not apply to the America represented by a Francie Dosson or an Isabel Archer or, as we shall presently see, a Strether and a Milly Theale. What this French view simply ignores is the identity of the moral sense with spontaneity and delicacy of the mind which is the most important characteristic of James's American heroines and heroes.

Even the joyous acceptance of life, the *joie de vivre,* is an integral part of James's American protagonists. It is evident in Christopher Newman; it is full blown in Isabel Archer's eagerness for experience; and if her eagerness has always a serious moral purpose, yet her enjoyment is by no means devoid of the sensuous. She is no cold moralist. But the relation between the moral intelligence and the fully lived life is a specific part of the theme of James's later novels. They continue his analysis of the contrast between American and European civilization on the lines established earlier, but with new discrimination. If the ambiguous decorum of the Proberts is the result of "long historical discipline," we have to go, therefore, to *The Ambassadors* to see what beauty that discipline could beget. If with the aid of "the grace of youth and innocence" Francie has once more attempted to convert "inconceivabilities of ignorance" into the "lively positives" of potential American strength, we have to go to *The Wings of the Dove* to see what this strength could amount to. And we have to go to *The Golden Bowl* to see what harmony of innocence and experience, of discipline and spontaneity, James could imagine.

IV

The Lesson of Social Beauty

ALTHOUGH James never lost his deep moral bias, the special value of his vision derives ultimately from his detachment from any one local point of view. This detachment prevented him from the kind of simplification which sees the world in black and white and led him finally to see the contrast between America and Europe in certain fundamental qualities which, not in themselves good or bad, contain the potentials for both. Ultimately this contrast came for him to lie in the very sources of moral judgment: in the difference between idealism and empiricism, between the laws of conduct which the individual derives from the sense of his independent relation to God and, on the other hand, the rules derived from the needs of social life and formalized in certain institutions and conventions of society. If he had come to see dangers inherent in the moral self-reliance of Americans, Europe had taught him not merely the reality of moral corruption which may be hidden under the decor of art and social form, but also the moral significance of style, beauty, order.

There is an early essay which shows how long James's final

point of view had been preparing. "If you have lived about," he wrote in 1878,

you have lost that sense of the absoluteness and the sanctity of the habits of your fellow-patriots which once made you so happy in the midst of them. You have seen that there are a great many *patriae* in the world, and that each of these is filled with excellent people for whom the local idiosyncrasies are the only thing that is not rather barbarous. There comes a time when one set of customs, wherever it may be found, grows to seem to you about as provincial as another.

"Compare then," he concluded, "as often as the occasion presents itself. The result as regards any particular people, and as regards the human race at large, may be pronounced agreeable, and the process is both instructive and entertaining."[1]

Occasion presented itself to James all his life, and the result of it is in his work. Finally he lost not only the smugness with which this early essay is touched, but his faith in the absoluteness of local values. Above all, international contrasts came to serve him as a means for exploring a more fundamental question—the nature of morality "as regards the human race at large." Yet, though the three climactic novels of his career—*The Wings of the Dove* (1902), *The Ambassadors* (1903), and *The Golden Bowl* (1904) —transcend what he called the *"emphasised* internationalism" of his early fiction, they nevertheless mark his return to the international scene. Though, as he said, a different setting might have served his thematic purpose in *The Ambassadors* if it could have represented "a place in which Strether's errand was likely to lie and his crisis to await him," Paris "had the great merit" of sparing him "preparations." Something like this is true of the other two novels of this period. Like *The Ambassadors,* they are concerned with a conflict between different moral sensibilities; and after years of expatriation James found such conflict most ready to his hand on the international scene. His sense of contrast—the kind of contrast on which, he felt, "any painter of life and manners inevitably much depends"—had been "rather oddly predetermined" for him by his "situation."[2] The consistency with which he arrayed various nationalities in his moral dramas is, therefore, neither incidental nor ephemeral. Taken together, the three novels form a trilogy exploring the possibilities of two radically different systems of morality represented by America and Europe. And coming just before his return to America in 1904, which led him to readjust his focus, they constitute a climax in his lifelong attempt to define his sense of the fundamental differences between the two worlds.

By this time, too, James had fully developed his late method: the author is abstracted from the text, and the story is wholly a story of individual consciousness—the characters' story of their story. Consequently, the international contrast has now ceased to be given in terms of an external conflict alone. Instead it is presented in terms of the growth of individual awareness—Strether's awareness of Parisian, Milly Theale's awareness of English, or Densher's of American modes of life. The novels, therefore, picture in the first place, not Europe and America, but the American experience of Europe, the European experience of America. They are novels of initiation and conversion and, in *The Golden Bowl,* finally, of fusion. Their very action consists in the apprehension of foreign modes of living, thinking, judging—a scheme which makes possible an analytical and comparative evaluation far more discriminating than anything in James's earlier work.

The first of James's novels to approach the international situation in this fashion was *The Ambassadors.*[3] Lambert Strether, the hero, is the one among all of James's important characters one is most tempted to identify with his author.[4] The reason is not far to seek: *The Ambassadors* is a story of the making of an American cosmopolitan and in this sense may be regarded as a kind of spiritual autobiography. The action is of course fictitious; in fact it has something of the fable or fairy tale, the form which more and more became James's medium for projecting what he saw as psychological and moral realities.

Strether, through whom the story is seen entirely, is a "man of imagination,"[5] and has therefore some of Isabel Archer's American virtue. But this is not "his prime faculty," nor is he presumptuous like her. He is a middle-aged man, and James "rejoiced," as he says, "in the promise of a hero so mature"; for Strether's highly developed "analytic faculty" enabled him to do what in *The Portrait of a Lady* he had left undone: though Isabel Archer's story is eminently the story of her disillusionment, we never see the growth of that disillusionment. At the end of Chapter XXXV we leave her engaged to Osmond; at the beginning of Chapter XXXVI she has been married to him for more than three years and is grimly undeceived. The break comes roughly in the middle of the novel, the first half serving to establish her romantic character and the second showing what the lesson of Europe has made of it. Only in the twenty pages of internal monologue which constitute Chapter XLII do we get a summary survey of the intervening years. The structure of *The Ambassadors* differs radically from this. The whole book is a kind of Chapter XLII, tracing the growth of the hero's perception step by step. Analysis in *The Portrait of a Lady*, moreover, has been primarily of the mind of the American heroine, of which the "Europe" of the American imagination forms a part; we have been interested primarily in what Isabel will *do*. In *The Ambassadors*, analysis is largely of the European scene itself; at the end Strether *sees*, and we are interested in *what* he sees. "The business of my tale and the march of my action, not to say the precious moral of everything," James says again, "is just my demonstration of this process of vision," and his emphasis falls both on *process* and on *vision*.

What is it that Strether sees? The answer to this question will show the relation between the themes of the lived life and of the lesson of Europe. About the theme of no other of his fictions did James commit himself so bluntly as about that of *The Ambassadors*. "Nothing is more easy than to state the subject"—thus his preface opens, and before the end of the page he has quoted Strether's crucial speech in Gloriani's garden in Chapter XI as an expression of "the essence" of the novel: "Live all you can; it's a mistake not to. It doesn't so much matter what you do in particular, so long as you have your life." The speech is too well known to be here quoted at length. This fragment, moreover, contains the essence of the whole, which is much more startling in isolation than when it is understood dramatically, as the speech must be understood. For James is of course far from advocating moral anarchy. Strether's case is, in the words of the preface, "comparative"—and comparative not merely with regard to Europe and America but at the same time with regard to the importance of doing and judging. What he comes to see is that in too much judging he has missed life. It is what with repeated emphasis he calls his past mistake, which is the mistake of Woollett, Massachusetts, for Strether is a product of "the very heart of New England." The crisis which leads to his lucidity is the "false position" in which he finds himself in Paris. He has come "primed with a moral scheme of the most approved pattern," approved, that is, in New England and hence "framed to break down on any approach to vivid facts," at least "to any at all liberal appreciation of them."[6]

The capacity for liberal appreciation is what distinguishes Strether from the rest of the Woollett clan. James calls *The Ambassadors* a "drama of discrimination," Strether's discriminations of course since all is seen as it reflects itself in his mind. But important among the things discriminated are various American attitudes toward Paris, beside Strether's own—whose changes constitute the action of the story—most important those of Chad Newsome and his sister Sarah Pocock, the latter representing Mrs. Newsome, their mother and Strether's friend, who is never present in person but throughout looms heavily as the purest and most potent source of the Woollett spirit. This latter attitude is what has brought Strether to Paris. He has come to rescue Chad, whom Woollett believes to be in the clutches of a Parisian enchantress. This view of Chad's imbroglio is very much what in the preface James calls "the dreadful little old tradition, one of the platitudes of the human comedy, that people's moral scheme *does* break down in Paris." It is the image of Paris as the "consecrated scene of rash infatuations," which in *The American* already he had felt to be a trap to be avoided by the novelist. So in *The Ambassadors,* the initiation of Strether into a mode of life radically different from that of Woollett "was to have nothing to do with any *bêtise* of the imputably 'tempted' state"—a fact which we shall have to remember when we come to consider the much disputed end of the novel. Instead, Strether was to be thrown "upon his lifelong trick of intense reflexion," which was to lead him a wonderful dance through winding passages of darkness and light to a realization of "more things than had been dreamt of in the philosophy of Woollett."[7] What happens to Strether is that he is thoroughly emancipated from the "dreadful little old tradition." What in the end he sees with a new clarity and sharpness of vision is not only Paris but Woollett itself, represented by the human symbols of Madame de Vionnet and Mrs. Newsome.

The problem confronting Strether is the question whether Chad's attachment to Madame de Vionnet represents, as Woollett believes, the breakdown of his morals or whether, as one of Chad's young friends tells Strether, it is "virtuous." The "virtuous attachment" becomes the focal point in which the various themes meet: the question of morality, the question of the lived life, and the international contrast. Strether's *volte-face* is made in a succession of two or three appraisals of what is appearance and what reality.

To summarize the sequence of his adjustments briefly, what strikes him at his very first meeting with Chad is a tremendous improvement in the young man's appearance. Instead of being coarsened by the process of sowing his wild oats, he seems of unexceptionable taste and manners, even of a dignity which can momentarily affect the older man with a kind of awe. Chad has simply been "made over," and the fact prepares Strether to believe that the attachment to Madame de Vionnet is "virtuous." Nor does this lady's own appearance in any way serve to dispel the impression. It is important that Strether first meets her in the garden of Gloriani, the distinguished sculptor, during a party in which the place, the assembled company, and even the soft spring afternoon, all conspire in an "assault of images" which brings to a sudden focus what has been growing in him almost from the moment he set foot on European soil—a new sense of life, a sense of "ease" before which his past life shows up as poverty-stricken. This is what provokes his sudden and ardent outburst. Yet, Strether's Woollett conscience is not dead. In the very current of his passionate appeal he realizes that he is "a case of reaction against the mistake," and that "the voice of reaction" must always be taken with an "allowance." What he remains concerned with is the reality hidden behind the brilliant show. Do these people all show "for what they really are?" he asks, only to have his seriousness laughed off as Christopher Newman already had his moral seriousness laughed off by Parisian "frivolity": "Oh, I like your Boston 'reallys'!"

At any rate, Strether's conclusion is that Chad's attachment to Madame de Vionnet *is* "virtuous." It is a pragmatic conclusion drawn from Chad's "improvement" and from Madame de Vionnet's own charm and beauty: "Ah, she was neither Turk nor Pole!" She is a *femme du monde* at the same time that she impresses Strether with her "common humanity." And like other Americans before him—Isabel Archer, for instance—Strether is moved to trust by the presence of a young daughter, a perfect *jeune fille* whose exquisite innocence testifies to the "tone" of the mother. In a word, Madame de Vionnet is simply the most exquisite of women. This is the view which Strether stoutly adheres to in the face of Sarah Pocock, the second Woollett ambassador sent out because Strether, the first, seems to falter in his mission. Sarah is not open to the appeal of the show, of appearances. Like Henrietta Stackpole in *The Portrait of a Lady*, though much less appealingly, she knows perfectly in advance what she will find in Europe. To her, Paris *is* the "consecrated scene of rash infatuations"; to her an attachment of a young American to a French woman is "wicked" by definition, since it is what the Woollett image of Paris prescribes. And the irony of Strether's predicament is that Sarah's view turns out to have been right as far as the mere physical facts are concerned. For the second step in Strether's initiation is his sudden discovery of what Chad's relations to Madame de Vionnet really are.

This of course is the crisis in Strether's education. Up to this point he has been concerned only with the appearance of things. He has argued against Sarah Pocock's crude assumption of Chad's corruption on the grounds of Madame de Vionnet's amiability, her rarity, her distinction—all his own words for describing her. And he has explained that to take a woman "at once so charming and so beneficent" for anything but what she appears, characterizes merely the Woollett state of mind, which proceeds "from our queer ignorance, our queer misconceptions and confusions," whereas he has found that "the proof of the pudding's in the eating"—a repudiation, this, of moral absolutism which, as he realizes immediately, cuts him off for good and all from Woollett. Sarah breaks with him, and he is left to cope alone with his last discovery that the particular "virtuousness" which he has come to believe in does after all not exist. For it *is* a discovery. Although to Sarah he has protested his right to think highly of Madame de Vionnet without investigating her actual "life," we find at the end that he has all along been taking the beauty of the surface for a positive sign of "virtuousness" in the literal Woollett sense of the word. His theory has been not only "that the facts were, specifically, none of his business" but that they "were, over and above, so far as one had to do with them, intrinsically beautiful."

His discovery that the relation of Chad and Madame de Vionnet is not what he had assumed, that—although for the wrong reasons —Woollett's estimate of the facts of this relationship has been accurate, comes therefore as a shock. "A sharp fantastic crisis," he feels, has suddenly "popped up," and what above all makes him feel it "as quite horrible" is the fact that Chad and Madame de Vionnet are clearly conscious of having something "to put a face upon." He finds that all along there has been "a *lie* in the charming affair," from the very moment when he was told that Chad's attachment to Madame de Vionnet was "virtuous." It is this "quantity of make-believe" which, as he ruminates on the compromising meeting he has had with the two lovers, most disagrees with "his spiritual stomach." But it is just this, too, which in the light of a new day ends by making the revolution in his moral thinking complete.

The setting where Strether realizes this is again significant. All through his adventure he has been much under the spell of the scenic frames of the people he has been concerned with. He has first met Madame de Vionnet in Gloriani's old garden among a company which has affected him like something of the "boundless menagerie" of which James speaks in the preface[8]—creatures beautifully plumed and "magnificently marked." He has seen her next in the deep "mildness and stillness" of her old house among her old possessions, which have spoken to him of "her rare unlikeness to the women he had known," of a beautiful passivity "under the spell of transmission," of "a deep suspicion of the vulgar," and of an "air of supreme respectability, the consciousness, small, still, reserved, but none the less distinct and diffused, of private honor." And finally, he has his sudden revelation of the facts of her relation to Chad in the French countryside, "a land of fancy for him—the background of fiction, the medium of art," and appealing quite particularly to him—thus James emphasizes Strether's response to the pictorial and associational—by reminding him of "a certain small Lambinet that had charmed him, long years before, at a Boston dealer's"—all of which has made the conditions of his meeting with the pair easy and natural and above all fundamentally different from the conditions of Woollett.

But the moment of his full awareness of what has happened to his moral sense comes on the morning following his night of lonely rumination. He is back in Paris, in the *Postes et Télégraphes* sending a reply to Madame de Vionnet's request to see him. And "the pressure of the place" again does its work, deciding him to see her once more in her home, "in her own best conditions." As he looks about himself at the little people scribbling messages, he realizes suddenly that he is "carrying on a correspondence, across the great city, quite in the key of the *Postes et Télégraphes* in general," and that accepting the fact as a matter of course, he is "mixed up with the typical tale of Paris." The realization amounts to an identification of himself with the Parisians: "they were no worse than he," and he "no worse than they—if, queerly enough, no better."

This last, that he should have arrived at a point where his moral superiority has vanished, is hard to swallow. An instinct in him still keeps him groping for some straw of "discipline" in "the silver stream of impunity" in which he feels himself floating with the rest of Paris. For a while he keeps reverting to the tradition he has been brought up in, which assumes that the "state" or at least the "happiness" of the "wrongdoer," presents some "special difficulty." But what strikes him above all now is the "ease" not only with which Chad and his lover have managed their affair but also with which he himself accepts the situation. The lesson of this ease is what finally puts the period to his whole education. "Their eminent 'lie,' Chad's and hers," this is where his ruminations finally lead him, is after all simply "such an inevitable tribute to good taste as he couldn't have wished them not to render." And he finally makes his way to Madame de Vionnet's house with the conviction that he can trust her "to make deception right." "As she presented things," he has learned, "the ugliness—goodness knew why—went out of them."

This is a far cry from the moral absolutism of Woollett—"to make deception right." Yet, it is what Strether comes out with. Even the friend who described Chad's relation to Madame de Vionnet as "virtuous" lied like a gentleman, showed him, Strether in fact now feels—and this without irony—"what's expected of a gentleman." For what has finally changed for Strether are the very criteria by which he determines what is "right" or "virtuous." That first lie was only "technical" since the attachment, quite regardless of certain facts, *is* virtuous because Madame de Vionnet is so. What this amounts to is that Strether has abandoned the moral "laws" of Woollett for some other criteria of what is "right," something which he can hardly name but which is represented for him by Madame de Vionnet's distinction, her charm, her amiability—qualities thrown vividly into relief by Sarah Pocock's and, as Strether comes to see, Mrs. Newsome's colder virtues. What has from the first acted as the wedge to loosen Strether's old beliefs has been his sense of the outward transformation of Chad. What makes him see virtue even in the affair as it is finally revealed to him is the person of Madame de Vionnet. Strether has quite simply become a pragmatist.

Yet Strether has abandoned none of his moral seriousness. What he has come to see is that the precepts of Woollett will not serve as guides for the moral evaluation of Paris, since they are part of the localism of manners and therefore subjective. The Woollett vision of Chad's imbroglio, from which Strether emancipates himself, is naïve, is a manifestation of the old American "innocence," though what James emphasizes this time is its negative aspect. It is peculiarly exposed to corruption for the very reason that it lacks the awareness which comes from experience. Sarah Pocock and Waymarsh, another New Englander "in the real tradition," have their "romance" together, affected by the "charged, infectious air" of the "classic ground," the "great temple" of pleasure which Paris is to them. Not to mention Jim Pocock, Sarah's husband, who—full of "innuendo as vague," Strether feels, "as a nursery-rhyme, yet as aggressive as an elbow in his side"—slyly envies Strether for having one more "good time" before it is too late and who spends his days sniffing up what he "supposes" to be Paris. Jim has his New England "categories in hand" and, despite his chummy sympathy for what he thinks of as Strether's and Chad's philandering, is therefore no less blind than the others—"stupid or wilful," as they strike Strether, in their inability to see Madame de Vionnet's real qualities. In accord with the Woollett view of Paris as the playground of errant husbands, Jim leaves the "moral side" of their adventure to his wife to the extent even of calling on Madame de Vionnet "all alone" at a time when Sarah makes no bones about what she thinks of "this person" and of "that sort of thing." And Strether indeed realizes that "he would have been held less monstrous had he only been a little wilder."

What all this comes to is that the whole Woollett tribe indulge their own pleasure and their own preconceptions. They all exemplify in their various ways what in the preface to *The Reverberator* James calls the "passionless pilgrims" among the Americans, who regarded Europe as a toy to be used and discarded at will. "A hundred good instances," James writes, "confirmed this tradition that nothing in the new world was held accountable to anything in the old,"[9] and in *The Ambassadors* he adds another half dozen illustrations or so to his collection. Even Chad—and this is the last irony in Strether's developing lucidity—turns out to be among them. For it becomes more and more clear that in the end he will after all return to Woollett and the family business, so that Strether, who has originally come out to "save" him from Madame de Vionnet, finds himself admonishing him: "You'll be a brute, you know—you'll be guilty of the last infamy—if you ever forsake her."

James's description of the "passionless pilgrims" contains in fact one sentence which applies to none of his characters as well as to Chad: "Europe," the "painted and gilded holiday toy," serves "its purpose on the spot and for the time" only "to be relinquished, sacrificed, broken and cast away, at the dawn of any other convenience."[10] What could describe better the "infamy" which Strether feels Chad subtly capable of? And what could be more ominous—particularly if we remember James's feelings about the vulgarity of modern publicity—than that the field in which Chad's new "convenience" seems to be dawning is the "science" of advertising? True, there are other suggestions: young Mamie has been brought over as a bait for him; and Strether half suspects "some other woman in London." But the note on which we see Strether and Chad separate for the last time, the fact that the latter has "encountered a revelation" in the "great new force of advertising"—in our "roaring age," he tells Strether, "an art like another"—and that this of all things is what finally kindles his interest in the Woollett business serves as an ominous climax to the various hints of vulgar insensitivity which Strether keeps hearing in the cavalier manner of Chad's allusions to Madame de Vionnet—a tone almost of street-corner swagger sometimes, which makes Chad's professions of faithfulness to her suspect by a too-much of protestation.

If Chad is going to cast off *his* "gilded holiday toy," it is not because of any European corruption.[11] It is, quite on the contrary, because in spite of all that Madame de Vionnet may have done for him, he still is "none the less only Chad," "*our* little Chad," as Strether elsewhere says with significant emphasis. The realization comes to him "with supreme queerness," and well it might. All his battle with Woollett has been an attempt to make them see that the Chad they meet in Paris is *not* "the same old Chad" they've been "glowering at across the sea," and now at the end he finds that he has been mistaken after all. The Chad who threatens to exchange Madame de Vionnet for the refinements of advertising, Strether realizes, is precisely the old Chad, and this last touch supplies the link which completes the chain of Strether's insights. For the last thing to which his eyes are opened is Woollett itself.

The most important symbol of Woollett is the distant figure of Mrs. Newsome, just as Madame de Vionnet is the most important symbol of Paris. And the transfer of Strether's allegiance from the one to the other is a token of his moral change of heart. His reassessment of Mrs. Newsome is pointed: *she* has not changed, she is "more than ever the same. But I do what I didn't before— I *see* her." The conversation in which this occurs points back explicitly to an earlier one, in which Strether's original vision of the lady is contained. There she rules over the family concern with "a delicacy and a discretion" beyond words, and after the fashion of the benevolent tycoon, she supports "as a tribute to the ideal" the green Review of which Strether is the editor. She is "a *moral* swell." At the end of his adventure Strether sees through all this. And though he does not formulate exactly what it is he sees, the accumulation of his thickening perceptions is clear enough.

Perhaps the most revealing of them comes half-way through the book. Strether has kept Mrs. Newsome religiously informed, has been in almost daily correspondence with her. But when he so obviously fails to return Chad to the bosom of Woollett, her letters stop, and it strikes him that he has "never so lived with her as during this period of her silence." This silence, more than anything else, expresses her to him—"so highly, so almost austerely, herself: pure and by the vulgar estimate 'cold,' but deep, devoted, delicate, sensitive, noble." Later, he himself is to judge her by the "vulgar estimate" when he realizes that the reason why Sarah can so effectively represent her is that "she's all cold thought" which can be served "cold without its really losing anything." That is, her virtues are not only ethereal, they are tenuous, to him who has come to see virtue more and more as a function of living. That her virtues—he comes to call them "idiosyncrasies"—should strike him most in her absence is symbolic of their divorce from the stuff of human contacts, a divorce which manifests itself in other ways, in what Strether comes to feel as "her want of tact" and above all in the moral obtuseness which makes her blind alike to Madame de Vionnet's beauty and to Jim Pocock's moral shabbiness. All this, as everything else in the novel, is Strether's point of view and merely indicates the change which has come over his sense of virtue. In his new vision, Mrs. Newsome's high idealism—for that is what it boils down to— takes on the color of the cold inhumanity which disturbs the reader in Euphemia de Mauves. Only, now the sense of the negative aspect is made more concrete—in those representatives of Woollett, Sarah and Jim and, after all, Chad.

The Ambassadors, then, is another version of the conflict between American and European manners, of American misapprehen-
sion of European conduct which had occupied James during his
earlier career. Unlike *The Portrait of a Lady,* a story of disenchantment which invokes our sympathy for American idealism, it is a
story of conversion. What we are asked to share is Strether's gradually growing awareness and finally his high sense of the moral
sufficiency of Madame de Vionnet, even of the moral beauty which
he comes to see in her despite her conflict with the moral regimen
of Woollett. Strether's final position is to some extent deterministic
as well as pragmatic, bound up as his judgment of Madame de
Vionnet is with the forces of tradition that have shaped her. In
Gloriani's garden he is explicit about this: "The affair of life," he
says, is

at the best, a tin mould, either fluted and embossed, with ornamental
excrescences, or else smooth and dreadfully plain, into which, a helpless
jelly, one's consciousness is poured—so that one "takes" the form, as
the great cook says, and is more or less compactly held by it: one lives,
in fine, as one can.

Evidently out of such considerations, James did what he could
to take the onus of what is technically adulterous from Madame de
Vionnet's relation to Chad by giving her a background strikingly
similar to that of Claire de Cintré in *The American.* Madame de
Vionnet has "been married, out of hand," to a "polished, impertinent
reprobate," whose brutality freed her entirely from the stigma of
marital failure: luckily, "he was so impossible that she had the
advantage of all her merits," she so amiable that "nobody had a
word to say" against her when she was forced to live separately
from him. All this is significant "history" to Strether and most significant the fact that Madame de Vionnet is part of an order "governed by such considerations as put divorce out of the question."[12]
What this contributes to the moral content of the novel is to free
Strether for the appreciation of Madame de Vionnet's virtues, which

to him prove themselves in the beauty which she salvages from the wreck of her life.

It is significant that in quoting Strether's climactic speech in the preface James omitted the emphatically deterministic parts. In spite of his awareness of the limitations of human freedom, he had temperamentally not a trace of the naturalist in him. Indeed, Strether's outburst ends in an assertion: "Still, one has the illusion of freedom"; therefore, "don't make *my* mistake. For it was a mistake. Live!" It is an assertion strikingly similar in tone to William James's famous challenge to his own doubts, and like it the necessary beginning of a search for moral clarification: "I will assume," William James had told himself, that free will "is no illusion. My first act of free will shall be to believe in free will." Neither Strether nor his author is of course a philosopher, yet one of William James's summaries of his own philosophy is a fit expression of their search for values: "My philosophy is what I call a radical empiricism," William James wrote in 1904, "which represents order as being gradually won and always in the making." It "rejects all doctrines of the Absolute." Similarly, Strether does not emancipate himself from his moral seriousness—any more than Emerson, for instance, in his revolt against dogmatism, denied the reality of moral distinctions. What his adventure teaches him is the fallibility of Woollett's "sacred rage" and, more important, the beauty of another mode of living—or, to borrow William James's words once more, the beauty of "the *attained* social character of European civilization."[13]

If Strether is no philosopher, he yet has the philosopher's love of truth. While the others are blinded by their preconceptions, while they make their beliefs subservient to their own desires, Strether's motives are quite impersonal. James emphasizes this by the question of Strether's marriage to Mrs. Newsome which constantly looms in the background as a potential motive. The task for which Strether has been sent to Paris resembles the traditional test which the fairy prince has to pass before he wins the hand of the princess. His returning Chad triumphantly to Woollett, he has more or less been given to understand, will be rewarded by the opening to him of the doors to Mrs. Newsome's heart. And as his moral exploration progresses, he comes to realize more and more that what it has been leading him away from is the safety not only of the Woollett creed but with it of an "opulent future" with Mrs. Newsome. But Strether scrupulously avoids being swayed by such personal considerations, and this precisely is part of his distinction. This is, as he realizes, "the refinement of his supreme scruple"—that he wishes to leave out of account what he himself may forfeit and to do everything for the sake of lucidity alone. It is why he leaves when Maria Gostrey, his mentor, falls in love with him and at the end all but offers herself as a substitute for the lady he has lost. Since it is his "only logic" not to have got anything for himself out of the whole affair, he must go "to be right."

The echo of Isabel Archer's final "as seems right" is striking, and Strether is indeed cousin-german to her. His vision was formed in Woollett, and he knows what inevitable cast that mold has given to the "helpless jelly" of his consciousness. Near the end, he sees himself under the likeness of "one of the figures of the old clock at Berne" which, when the hour strikes, come out to jig along "their little course in the public eye"—and the image, once more sounding the note of his determinism, has a part in what makes for his final decision. Once more, too, the temptation to speak of Strether's experience as a fable dramatizing James's own is great—not only because James could at times speak of his own situation as an accident imposed upon him. More important, if Strether despite his moral revolution retains an eye for what "makes" him right almost puritan in its "horrible" sharpness, James, too, despite expatriation, never lost the deep moral bias of his origins.

But the real reasons for Strether's tacit rejection of Maria Gostrey's tacit proposal are part of the dramatic structure of the novel. For one thing, his taking his ease at her inn would obfuscate the clear line between his impersonal motives and the Woollett conception of them, since Woollett, too, might conclude that "the proof of the pudding's in the eating." It would bring Strether dangerously close to the *"bêtise* of the imputably 'tempted' state," and this at a time when his unselfishness is more than ever important as a foil to Chad's egotism. Above all, however, Strether is more deeply moved by Madame de Vionnet than he quite realizes. To the end, she is to him "the finest and subtlest creature, the happiest apparition" it has been given him to meet. And it is this sense more than anything else that puts an end to Maria Gostrey's hopes. The contrast between these two women, too, is part of Strether's growing discrimination. Settling down to a comfortable old age among Maria Gostrey's "specimens" of crockery and silver and pewter would be a mere taking refuge from the fulness of his knowledge. For he has learned to distinguish between the items of her "little museum of bargains" and Madame de Vionnet's "quite different" relics, which speak to him not of the rummaging, exchanging, selecting of the "contemporary method of acquisition" but of the beautiful and quiet "spell of transmission" from one generation to the next and therefore of an order more private, more dignified and substantial than Maria's.

This contrast—similar to the one between Osmond and Warburton in *The Portrait of a Lady*—goes to the heart of the international theme of *The Ambassadors.* As the *Notebooks* show, James had found the germ of his story in a reported glimpse of Howells in Paris, "virtually in the evening" of his life and sadly aware of being too old to take advantage of what he saw for the first time.[14] But what the "little situation" turned into was a drama not merely of the loss of experience but of the gain of knowledge. And though Maria Gostrey has been Strether's mentor, he, the pupil, has outdistanced her. "He has come so far through his total little experience that he has come out on the other side—on the other side, even, of a union with Miss Gostrey"—this is the way James put it in the long preliminary statement which he submitted to his publisher as a "project" of the novel. Strether's experience has made him "so quite other that, in comparison, marrying Miss Gostrey would be almost of the old order," and "their lingering, ripe separation" must therefore be "the last note."[15]

All this goes to say that if there is something tragic in Strether's life, it is not so much what he has missed as what he has learned. It is contained in his picture of Madame de Vionnet. For what he comes to see with a final shock is that the woman whose deep beauty is the main cause of his new vision is after all not proof against defeat and pain. He is amazed to find that *she* should be "down in the dust," and "put there by *our* little Chad." This is the only trace left here of James's earlier theme of the pretense of aristocracy, but how transformed it now is! What shocks Strether is not the artificiality of an institution which was the lesson of, say, Euphemia de Mauves's discovery of her husband's libertinism. It is the much profounder shock of seeing into the very depths of common human weakness. James avails himself of all the suggestive power of Shakespeare's Cleopatra when Strether can "think of nothing but the passion, mature, abysmal, pitiful" betrayed by the spectacle of the rare creature troubled as vulgarly "as a maidservant crying for her young man." Only, what distinguishes Madame de Vionnet in her prostration is that she judges herself as the maidservant would not, and the "weakness" of her "wisdom," Strether feels, seems but "to sink her lower"—which more than anything perhaps shows how far his experience has taken him from the moral thinking of Woollett.

Strether's new vision consists in the awareness that there is a virtue which cannot be measured by the bundle of moral "notions with which he started from home." One of the convictions which thicken for him in the course of his adventure is indeed a sense of the high value which the relation with a woman like Marie de Vionnet represents "for any young man." But if the revisions he has to make in his moral assumptions are "almost grotesque," that is merely so because they land him in a fundamental contrast between civilizations, between "the special phase of civilization" embodied by the "bustling business at home, the mercantile mandate, the counter, the ledger, the bank, the 'advertising interest,'" and the civilization for whose "charm" Madame de Vionnet comes to stand. This summary of the "core of the subject" is James's own in his preliminary "project," and it ends with the explicit statement that Strether's story amounts to a moral reconsideration of civilization.[16]

But it must not be understood that *The Ambassadors* represents James's last word on the subject, nor that *The Wings of the Dove* and *The Golden Bowl,* which followed it, constitute progressive revisions of his views. If the idealization of Madame de Vionnet is, in the light of his earlier handling of the American girl, rather striking, the reason is simply that here his emphasis falls on the possibilities of social discipline and experience rather than on the promise of innocence and spontaneity. In these novels, James was much less interested in making final value judgments than in exploring the origins and possibilities of contrasting modes of moral life, and this precisely is his most important contribution to the American genre of international fiction. It is a contribution inseparable from his concern with individual consciousness. In these three novels, therefore, he analyzed the awareness which the social conflict between America and Europe brings to various representatives of either side. *The Ambassadors* traces the growth of such awareness in the mind of an American, *The Wings of the Dove* and *The Golden Bowl,* as we shall see, in the representatives of the European order as well. "The consequences of the cosmopolite spirit," he had written in that early essay with which this chapter opens, "is to initiate you into the merits of all peoples." And what stands out in these late works is the idealization of different kinds of merit: of social beauty in Madame de Vionnet, of a high spiritual beauty in Milly Theale, and of their fusion in the marriage of Maggie Verver and the Roman Prince in *The Golden Bowl.*

V

The Lesson of Spiritual Beauty

THEMATICALLY, *The Wings of the Dove* is a companion piece to *The Ambassadors*. In both novels the international contrast is an integral part of the theme of the lived life. Both show the exposure of American innocence to a knowing Europe, but with a different critical focus. While the Paris of the first represents the beautiful order which results from a continuity of social experience, the second is concerned with the corruption, the perversion of motives attendant upon the process of refinement when social organization becomes subservient to greed. In a sense, therefore, *The Wings of the Dove* is a return to an earlier contrast; yet in spite of certain similarities, it is thematically no mere new version of *The Portrait of a Lady*.

The most obvious difference from that earlier novel is that the expatriate snob has left the picture so that the conflict is now entirely between America and Europe proper. More important and at first sight more puzzling, James's sympathies here are much less clearly placed: at the same time that Milly Theale, the American heroine, is highly idealized, her European antagonists, though brutal in their greed, are not simply condemned. The reason is that while *The Portrait of a Lady* was written primarily from the point of view of Isabel, while it is almost purely a story of the American experience of "Europe," *The Wings of the Dove* is both that and, even more, the story of the European experience of America. It is written from, fundamentally, two points of view—Milly's and Merton Densher's, the Englishman's. Milly's, though, is supplemented by that of her American companion, Susan Stringham, whose function as a "choral" *ficelle* is to supply "an *animated* reflexion of Milly Theale's experience of English society,"[1] to give what Milly herself would give if she were less purely spirit incarnate. *The Wings of the Dove,* then, just as much as *The Ambassadors,* avoids the "platitude of statement" and instead gives two versions of the story which is its physical action.

This is why in spite of so shabbily sordid a plot it is so subtle a book. What matters is not the physical action but the gradual revelations which it brings to Milly and above all to Densher. Hence the stylistic peculiarities: the lyrical and reflective passages in which the physical action is veiled, the fact that there are memories of conversations almost more than actual conversations. Hence also the structural peculiarity which results in an ambiguity easily misunderstood: the fact that we never get inside Kate Croy, the third major character, who is almost totally responsible for the physical action. Kate is tremendously present as a force, a form, a beautiful apparition, "the handsome girl," as Milly keeps thinking of her—a symbol of the English society which is the subject of Milly's fascinated observation and from which Densher finally emancipates himself thanks to the light which Milly has thrown on it for him. Kate in fact is all action, while Milly is spiritual sufferance and Densher physical response and finally intellectual rejection. Kate acts, Milly is, Densher judges. The relations between the three make up the substance of the story, and the peculiar "difficulty" of the book is that Kate, whose personal "story" the reader does not get except in so far as he gets it through the "fusion" of her consciousness with Densher's,[2] is the most vivid fact in the stories of the others and through them in the reader's mind.

Kate, then, is the one who creates the physical action. But the germinal idea, as the *Notebooks* show, was in the character and predicament of Milly—in the words of James's preface, "a young person conscious of a great capacity for life" but early stricken by a fatal disease and "passionately desiring" to achieve before her death, "however briefly and brokenly, the sense of having lived."[3] Milly's striking curiosity about London society, about people she does not know and has no specific motive for wishing to know, is a symbolic manifestation of her eagerness for experience, a desire which her involvement with Kate and Densher more than fulfils.

In his preliminary notes James envisaged that, moved by the pathos of her situation, Densher would devote himself to Milly for wholly charitable reasons, that with the sympathetic consent of his lover, Kate, he would "show her some delicacy of kindness," and that a dramatic complication would result from the tension between Kate's magnanimity and her awakening jealousy.[4] As he developed his "action," however, Densher's and Kate's motives changed, and in the final execution Densher is the pliable and for a long time blind instrument of a design of Kate's which is an ambiguous mixture of charity and greed. Since Milly is in love with Densher, thus Kate calculates, she will doubtless leave him her fortune and thus make possible his marriage to Kate, which "poverty" so far prevents. Their engagement, Kate's and Densher's, therefore is to be kept secret. On this plan they proceed with success until Lord Mark, a disappointed suitor for Kate's as well as Milly's favor, guesses their game and informs Milly. This is the essence of the experience which England supplies for Milly, and the shock of the discovered deception breaks her will to live—the will which alone has kept her from succumbing to her fatal illness.

It is, however, not the final consummation of her experience. In outlining his action, James briefly stumbled on the difficulty of imagining a conclusion that would not be "ugly and vulgar." But he saw the difficulty only to find immediately a way out: the saving turn was to make the happiness, the snatched experience Milly longs for *be* "some act of generosity, of passionate beneficence, of pure sacrifice, to the man she loves"—be, in fact, "something fine and strange."[5] Thus James planned it in *The Notebooks;* and in the finished novel, though from the moment she is aware of the betrayal Milly, as far as we are allowed to know, feels nothing but the deepest pain, pain at the loss of love and life together, yet the last note is that of her magnanimity, the virtue which shines most blindingly now that it knows of evil. She is indeed a transfiguration of the American girl. It is as if someone had said to James, "It is easy for these American girls to be so pure when they lack experience," and as if he had answered, "Ah, but see how far and straight they will go even when they know. Why, knowing the world will show up their moral beauty only the more splendidly!" As far as *The Wings of the Dove* is Milly's story it is a peculiarly American tragedy, the ravishment of innocence, of moral beauty, by a worldliness so knowing that it has forgotten the knowledge of innocence.

This is, however, less than half the story, for Milly's drama becomes the drama of Kate Croy and above all of Merton Densher too. As they use her for interests of their own, we see them, in the words of James's preface, "inheriting from their connexion with her strange difficulties and still stranger opportunities"; above all we see Densher "confronted with rare questions and called upon for new discriminations," as a result of which the "success" of their scheme is of no use to them;[6] for as Kate puts it at the last, they are not as they were before. Densher is possessed by his memory of Milly and therefore willing to marry Kate only on condition that they give up Milly's millions and only for the sake of his loyalty to Kate—bases, both, which Kate cannot accept, so that the end, in spite of the total success of their common enterprise, finds them ironically separated as nothing has been able to separate them before. In a word, Densher has been "bribed away" from the orbit of his previous life.[7]

Though it is not the only way in which the novel can be read, to read it as the story of Densher's changing relations to Milly and Kate is the most direct way to the general design which underlies the surface of changing points of view. A skeleton plot almost of the nature of the fairy tale or the morality play suggests the struggle of the good and the bad princess for mastery of the prince, of the good and the bad angel for possession of the soul of man—an allegorical framework suggested by the white and black in which Milly and Kate are clothed and by certain scattered passages reminiscent of biblical imagery. There is, for instance, Susan Stringham's early view of Milly on a high Alpine mountainside, which looks like a composite allusion to two of Christ's temptations. Already filled with a sense of her doom, Milly is "deeply and recklessly meditating." But she is "not meditating a jump"; on the contrary, in a state of "unlimited possession" that has "nothing to gain from violence," she is "looking down on the kingdoms of the earth," and Susan asks herself whether she is choosing among them or whether she wants them all. The reader is left in suspense. And indeed it is unlikely that James intended anything more specific than to give the dramatic figure of Milly an extension reaching beyond the world of New York millionaires—the same kind of extension that he confers upon her "high, dim, charming, ambiguous oddity" by making her impress people again and again with her princeliness. What Susan Stringham brings away from her vision, at any rate, is the conviction that the future is "not to exist for her princess in the form of any sharp or simple release from the human predicament," but that it will be "a question of taking full in the face the whole assault of life." This near the beginning, immediately following the picture of Kate's and Densher's eminently human world. It points across the whole book to the end where Kate realizes for Densher, with the penetration which is typical of her, that Milly has died *for* him that he "might understand her"—a formulation which makes the reader wonder whether he is perhaps *not* going too far in being reminded of another prince, the Prince of Peace, who too had no "quick escape" but drank the full measure of his cup and died that men might understand.

Densher himself is certainly touched by such intimations of something otherworldly when after Milly's death he sees himself "in a relation inconceivable," "hushed, passive, staying his breath, but half understanding, yet dimly conscious of something immense." He feels that something has happened to him "too beautiful and too sacred to describe," that he has been "forgiven, dedicated, blessed." And he knows that it is not by accident that the final token of Milly's forgiveness comes to him on Christmas morning, bringing him a "sense of that marked element of the rare" which he feels to be "the sign of his crisis." This revelation completes his emancipation from the arms of Kate, from the force of his own passion for the beautiful woman. For it has been his uxoriousness, the inevitable "abjection of love," as he calls it, which first made him submit blindly to Kate's unrevealed plan and which has kept him in subjection to her even when he has come to know it and to question its ethics. As a result, the passion responsible for the grow-ing "aggravation of his inward sense" of falseness turns into a mere means of escape from that sense; it becomes "their final remedy, the need to bury in the dark blindness of each other's arms the knowledge of each other that they couldn't undo." The knowledge which has destroyed their Eden forces Densher, in contrast to Adam, to abandon his Eve since she will not accept the new dispensation.

Such passages, allusions, overtones give the book a dimension far beyond that of any of James's other international dramas. They are related to the difficulty which some readers find in the figure of Milly, to the fact that, though the heroine, she is for more than the last fifth of the whole novel present only as a reflected image so that even certain highly climactic scenes, like Densher's leavetaking of her, are not enacted. The reason for this indirection is simply that in the moral scheme of the novel Milly finally has to undergo a kind of transfiguration, both the pain and the sublimity of

which are beyond dramatic representation. She has felt the fearful-
ness and the trembling out of which the Psalmist sang, "Oh that I
had wings like a dove! for then would I fly away, and be at rest."
And Kate and Densher finally have only the image of the spreading
wings of the dove to express their sense of what Milly has done to
them.

Indeed, much earlier Kate has thought of Milly in her innocence
and meekness as a dove, and the realization of the power finally
revealed under the image comes to her with something of a shock,
which the irony of her phrasing shows: "I used to call her, in my
stupidity—for want of anything better—a dove. Well she stretched
out her wings, and it was to *that* they reached. They cover us." It
is part of Kate's own power that she yet does not submit to what she
acknowledges—part of the unregenerate consistency of the black
angel, which distinguishes her from the weakness of man that is
Densher's salvation, and which makes her throughout the novel so
vivid a presence that her dark beauty almost overshadows Milly's
pure white.

This, however, only serves James's major purpose. For *The
Wings of the Dove* is no allegory on a biblical subject. It is a drama
not of unambiguous conflict between heaven and hell, but of the
contrast between two kinds of human ethics. What the biblical
overtones and symbols suggest is the extreme to which the contrast
between Milly's unencumbered spirit and Kate's "talent for living"
can be reduced philosophically—the contrast between the simplicity
of American idealism and the complexity of English empiricism.
Here, in contrast with *The Ambassadors*, James focuses on the
purity of the first and the dubiety of the second; but it must always
be remembered that the drama, as in *The Ambassadors* almost
wholly internal, is a drama of mutual initiation: Milly's into the
ambiguous "quantities" of the "accumulated contents" of English
social organization, and Densher's into the possibilities of a totally
different mode of conduct. For the evaluation, mutual also, takes
place entirely in the individual consciousness. In particular, the high

idealization of Milly is in large part of Densher's doing, is part of his emotional response to the dramatic circumstances of his involvement in the conflict between the two civilizations.

Densher's story can be summarized as the story of his conversion from the worship of Kate to the worship of Milly, based on a process of gradually deepening vision which is the counterpart of Strether's. But the process is much less simple and clear than the terms to which it finally leads him. In the preface to *The Portrait of a Lady* James speaks of the "dependence of the 'moral' sense of a work of art on the amount of felt life concerned in producing it."[8] The felt life which projects James's moral sense in *The Wings of the Dove* is above all the felt ambiguity of the choices Densher is confronted with. Densher's crisis is the direct result of his involvement with Kate, but it arrives only when he has finally become aware of Kate's scheme—"Since she's to die I'm to marry her?" Densher has asked. "So that when her death has taken place I shall in the natural course have money?" "You'll in the natural course have money," Kate has answered. "We shall in the natural course be free" to marry. But the execution of the scheme is up to Densher alone; Kate refuses to go into the details of that: "from the moment you don't wash your hands of me," she tells him, "you must act as you like and as you can." With this, after Kate has sealed the bargain by spending a night with him, Densher is left alone with Milly in Venice and the book is from here on almost exclusively the story of the education of his conscience.

What he is faced with is not a simple moral choice between good and bad, but a dual dilemma. Loyalty to Kate, which by her surrender to him has become a moral obligation in addition to being an inclination, is in conflict with his sense of decency. Even more problematic, honesty toward Milly is in conflict with kindness toward her, since what has kept her alive has been the will to live for his love. So that for the sake of kindness to Milly as well as of loyalty to Kate, Densher feels himself forced to play the thoroughly equivocal game. Yet he squirms under his sense of the falseness of his relation to Milly. It drives him to strange moral accommodations. He perceives that if he can still feel that his relation to Milly is "innocent," it is Milly herself who has purged it. Something in her national character, "the great national, the great maidenly ease" of the American girl is a "boon inappreciable." Something incalculable in that, he feels, works for him and Kate, "something outside, beyond, above themselves, and doubtless ever so much better, than they"—to this he keeps coming back—makes for "daily decency."

Milly herself, "divine in her trust" or "inscrutable in her mercy," as she strikes Densher, is aware of this, though not of the pointed irony her comment has for Densher's ears when she says, "you like us to be as we are because it's a kind of facilitation to you that we don't quite measure: I think one would have to be English to measure it!" With this fragment of remembered conversation Densher remembers also that strangely enough Milly has said it "without prejudice to her good nature." Yet with all this, Densher can still feel that not to profit by Milly's good nature would be to go directly against it, and that "the spirit of generosity" which it engenders in him could feel "no greater pang than by his having to go directly against Milly." Thus he temporizes, and whatever doubts he may still have about the dishonesty of his procedure he muffles with the idea of "tact," the virtue of "the sensitive and the kind." He is not "inhuman," he assures himself, so long as "tact" will serve. And for three weeks he can feel that tact and the simple intention to be kind—with the help, to be sure, of the incalculably purifying air of Milly's disposition—are sufficient guides by which to steer his course.

How long they might have thus served neither Densher nor the reader knows. At the end of the period, at any rate, he finds that Milly will not receive him and his sense of smooth sailing immediately deserts him. Loyalty to Kate and kindness to Milly have indicated the same course, but since loyalty to Kate reminds him inevitably of the lie in his kindness to Milly, his *modus vivendi* has been to keep the two apart, to keep the sense of Kate shut away in his rooms, where the memories of her surrender and quittance linger "as an obsession importunate to all his senses." Now, with Milly withdrawn, Kate reasserts herself with the result of his seeing himself as Kate's agent, a view which makes him immediately sensitive to the light in which Milly's servants have been seeing him—as a simple fortune hunter. It is, Densher feels, a vulgar view because it is the view which "might have been taken of an inferior man." Still, he knows that "the particular attribution of motive" does him after all no wrong. This is the beginning of a series of moral perceptions which are to lead him finally to abandon Kate, but for the time being he still clings to his disbelief in his own wrong.

That all has turned dismal, he can momentarily feel as "part of his punishment" until the sudden accidental sight of Lord Mark once more comes to the aid of his need for self-justification. If Milly will not receive him, if the rain is ugly, the wind wicked, if in a word vice is in the air, it is *"because* of Lord Mark." Densher senses that Lord Mark must have undeceived Milly and, ironically, from this very recognition can derive a sense of his own blamelessness, since what must have been the brutality of the other's revelation is precisely what he himself has so studiously avoided. Yet he cannot quite escape the sense of odium, the odium at least which must attach to him in the eyes of others; and his only gesture toward decency is, again ironically, a breach in kindness—the determination to stay near Milly in spite of his belief that now she probably wants him to go. To stay in spite of this, in spite of odium, in spite perhaps of some final experience that may be all but unbearably painful, he feels, is a way "to mark his virtue beyond any mistake," since, showing that he accepts the disagreeable, it will be "proof of his not having stayed" for the money. All of this chapter (XXX) is thus given to Densher's ineffectual manipulation of his moral dilemma in the privacy of his own soul. But at the end Susan Stringham comes to speak to him of Milly, and with her the reality of Milly's situation enters the rooms where his memories of Kate have been shut away and puts an end to his sophistications.

"She has turned her face to the wall"—in these words Susan immediately confronts him with the terror of that reality. Milly is grim, she is dying. Once this is out, Susan treats Densher gently. He sees—for everything is Densher's vision to the end—that she has come to pity rather than to judge him. She neither accuses him, nor does he confess. She merely asks that he deny what must have been Lord Mark's accusation. Later sending for him, Milly herself gives him an opportunity for such a denial, but we never witness that last scene between them. We never see Milly in the hour of her greatest need and her greatest power. What they must have been, however, we amply gather from the impact they have on Densher.

The last hundred pages of the novel, concerned entirely with his relation to Kate, end in their final separation. For Densher everything now is changed, and most of all Kate. In Venice his sense of what she had done for him by her physical surrender had already incurred a qualification: he came to feel that in returning to London Kate provided for her own "ease" while leaving him "peculiarly alone." Now, at his first reunion with her in London, he wonders at once whether he is "as different for her" as she immediately appears to him. Now, too, we find out that he has not been able to deny Lord Mark's accusation. "If I had denied you," he tells Kate, "I would have stuck to it." "You'd have 'chucked' me"—she sees it perfectly—"to save your conscience?" The "talent for life" which Densher has so often admired in her is still paramount; but now, in spite of her dignity, it strikes him, as it never struck him before, "as glib." And the total divergence of their vision becomes clear, to Densher and the reader, in the conclusion of their interview. Kate finds that Milly has had the "peace of having loved," of having *"all"* she wanted"—she pronounces it with customary lucidity and authority. "We've succeeded," for Milly "won't have loved you for nothing," and "you won't have loved *me*." The pragmatic judgment of values which in *The Ambassadors* is Strether's virtue has in Kate's view of Milly's death turned cruelly utilitarian. Densher, whose "aftersense" of that death, of Milly's pain and the magnanimity with which she surmounted it, is now "his greatest reality," winces under the dreadful irony of Kate's words. Her "brightness" chills him; more and more her "lucidity" horrifies him. He has been motivated all along by his passion for her, and now in the dawn of "mere cold thought" he comes to see that all along she has confused love with money.

The conflict between Kate's frigid materialism and Densher's awakened sense of the spirit is brought to its logical conclusion by a dramatization in which every inflection of the voice counts. Since their "dreadful game" has all been to make their marriage possible, Densher now feels that they can save a remnant of their self-respect only by marrying without waiting another day; Kate, in her "imperturbable consistency," must wait until the money is in the bag, for "I don't see, you know," she says, "what has changed." Or, Kate burns unread the last letter from Milly which Densher has handed over to her in token of their mutual confidence; for again, what matters to her is not the personal testament "sacred" to Densher but the material substance of the will which Milly's solicitor can communicate. Hence, "You'll have it all," she says to Densher, "from New York." To the end she is in full control. When Densher finally presents her with a choice between his love and Milly's money, she tells him that only his word of honor that he is not in love with Milly's memory will save him from her choice of the money. Her condition once more betrays all her "talent for life." For she well knows that with his memory of Milly's unearthly magnanimity, Densher is unfit for the great worldly marriage she wants. The man who has had the terrible sight of Milly's "consciously and helplessly dying," who has seen "the great smudge of mortality across the picture" of her passionate "dream of a future," cannot continue in acquiescent community with a world which seems to live in pointed ignorance of that last knowledge.

So much for Densher's conversion. It remains to show that Milly and Kate are representative of the civilizations which have formed them. Something of Densher's and Milly's sense of the matter we have seen already, but there is more. In the preface, for instance, grouping Milly with the Daisy Millers, James explains that Milly's predicament provided a chance to confer upon the type of the American girl "a supremely touching value"[9]—which may serve as a summary of the gradual transformation of Densher's vision of Milly. At first, she is to him simply "little Miss Theale," the typical American girl, one of the "many little Miss Theales" he has seen in New York, one of "the irrepressible, the supereminent young persons" who strike the Englishman as a typical American phenomenon. At the end, she has become "supremely touching," has in Densher's vision indeed acquired what Howells once described as "the charming and honorable distinctions of American girlhood" which demonstrated for Europe "a civilization so spiritual that its innocent daughters could be not only without the knowledge but without the fear of evil."[10] James himself would doubtless have found this manner of putting it too naïve for unqualified assent. But it is not far from what Densher sees in Milly, and both the novel and the preface emphasize her national character.

If Milly is in a sense typical, so is Kate. Both personify the moral bases of their native civilizations. For Kate this means a world in which conduct is governed not by objective principle but by subjective interest. As she explains to Milly at one point, in England "every one who had anything to give—it was true they were the fewest—made the sharpest possible bargain for it, got at least its value in return"; and remembering the statement later, Milly finds it only the stranger that all this can amount to the "happy understanding" of a social system whose wheels are so "wonderfully oiled." Of this world all of Milly's new English friends are part, and each for private reasons of his own contributes to the conspiracy against her—which is the reason why Densher finally measures the odium of his weakness by the fact that he has pleased everybody. It is the reason also why he can make himself understood to Kate's wealthy aunt Maud no more than to Kate herself. Aunt Maud, he feels, responds to the tale of his revelation very much "as a stout citizen's wife" might respond to a tear-jerker, with "why in pity" should she not have lived, "with everything to fill her world? The mere *money* of her, the darling, if it isn't too disgusting at such a time to mention that—!" Across this gulf communication is impossible. For as Milly has put it, with nothing but "the finest outward resonance," these people are "familiar with everything, but conscious, really of nothing"; they lack—and she has used James's own old term—"imagination."

The fundamental contrast between Milly and the England of her abysmal experience is elaborated in a multitude of ways, but dramatized most pointedly through Kate. Kate has representative value because, as James shows with meticulous care, her character and conduct are determined largely by the circumstances of her life —the monstrous caddishness of her flashy father, the sordid squalor of her sister, the vulgar opulence of her aunt Maud, who frees her from poverty only to enslave her by the strong appeal of "material things." The unmitigated materialism of her environment is the ultimate cause of her disfigurement, the reason why her great gift, her splendid "talent for life," turns into the simple "greatness of knowing" what she wants, and finally into something which can be called talent only with the bitterest of ironies or the most cold-blooded of cynicisms. Nothing makes the deep perversion of her sense of values more painfully clear than that she makes a virtue of subordinating her passion for Densher to her passion for wealth: she does not like his courting of Milly but, she tells him, "when you know me better you'll find out how much I can bear." The irony of it becomes clear to the reader only when he too knows her better. She can, indeed, bear too much; for the sake of the "great" future, she can do violence to the integrity of her own feelings. Her deep corruption lies in the *use* she makes of her own love and of her own great endowments, in her *abuse* of one sort of value for ends of quite another sort.

Yet, to the very end one is aware of James's sympathy for the dark brilliance of Kate's presence, a sympathy almost reminiscent

of his feelings for some quite different children of his imagination
—for Isabel Archer, for example, and *her* mistaken belief in the
sufficiency of her own mind and will, or for Strether and his sense
that life could not have been different for him. For Kate is not a
free agent either. If her "talent" is all her own, she has not chosen
the channels into which it has been forced. Even Milly raises the
question of free will. One day, as she sits on one of the benches in
Regent's Park, she sees herself "in the same box" with the multi-
tudes around her, the box of the "great common anxiety," of "the
practical question of life." Like herself, those "hundreds of others"
have doubtless been told that "they could live if they would," a
piece of information, she comes to feel, which strangely merges into
"the blessed old truth that they would live if they could." Finally
she feels that there is little to choose between the two faces of the
question: it is "perhaps superficially more striking that one could
live if one would," but it is "more appealing, insinuating, irresistible,
in short, that one would live if one could." Highly unusual, this
near-identification of two views of life usually thought of as irrec-
oncilably opposed to one another. And one wonders whether
Milly's final magnanimity is perhaps in part a recognition of the
fact that Kate and Densher, too, live not so much as they will but
—in Strether's phrase—as they can,[11] as England has taught them.

That James lets even Milly thus meditate, that he lets her see
her "ultimate state" as that of "a poor girl—with her rent to pay,"
explains perhaps—as Strether's vision of Marie de Vionnet's abasement does in *The Ambassadors*—the coexistence of judgments
grown from the belief in the sovereign power of the spirit and
judgments grown from the sense of a necessity in human affairs.
But though necessity makes Kate and Milly sisters in suffering, it
does not void moral judgment here any more than it does in *The
Ambassadors,* and this fact puts a final emphasis on their significance
as national symbols. The difference between Kate and Milly is the
difference between the civilizations which have molded them.
Nothing, finally, strikes Densher more than the moral inadequacy

of the civilization which has led him and Kate into the "dreadful game" they have played for Milly's money with Milly's life. He has, James tells us, a "vivid mental image" for this difference: the more he realizes their common abjection, the more urgent is his need of being at least absolutely "straight" with Kate. But "straightness" is the honesty of thieves, the virtue of an order in which no one does anything for nothing, and it turns morally stale on his hands. His one act of disloyalty to Kate, a secret exchange of letters with Susan Stringham about Milly's memory, therefore comes to appear to him "as a small emergent rock in the waste of waters, the bottomless grey expanse of straightness." And the lesson he finally draws is that for "daily decency" the well-oiled social mechanism of which they have been part needs something "beyond and above" itself. Even at best, it is a mere gray watery waste, in which the emergent rock of the spirit alone can give a sense of moral security. With this final image Densher's conversion from the cunning of the serpent to the wisdom of the dove is defined.

Like *The Ambassadors,* then, *The Wings of the Dove* is a story of conversion. But the direction is reversed. Whereas the first dramatizes the values of empirically derived forms of conduct by contrast with the pitfalls of moral absolutism, the second dramatizes the insufficiency of any moral knowledge purely empirical, *its* liability to corruption, by contrast with an image of supreme spiritual beauty. *The Golden Bowl,* as we shall now see, images a synthesis. If the first two novels of the trilogy are dramas of conversion, the last is the drama of a double conversion and finally achieved harmony.[12]

VI "Sublime Consensus"

AN AWARENESS of the thematic unity of the three novels James wrote around the turn of the century contributes greatly to the understanding of his intent in *The Golden Bowl*. The character of Adam Verver and his relation to Maggie has repeatedly given rise to difficulties which can be overcome when the place of this novel in the canon of James's international fiction is recognized—when Adam Verver is seen for what, historically, he is: another of the "passionless pilgrims,"[1] as James called them, cousin-german to Chad Newsome of *The Ambassadors,* and almost something of the villain of the drama. For in the marriage of Maggie Verver and Prince Amerigo, *The Golden Bowl* symbolizes a union of America and Europe which becomes real only when it has purged itself of irresponsibility—particularly of the American irresponsibility toward Europe represented by Adam Verver. Essentially, *The Golden Bowl* is a prophetic fable, prefiguring a "sublime consensus," the fusion of two points of view which in its companion pieces in the trilogy remain unreconciled.

Physical action and character cast in *The Golden Bowl* are

quite in the tradition of James's previous international fiction. The action, revolving around the usual international marriage, begins with the betrayal of an innocent American girl by a European aristocrat—that is, with a situation not unlike the one at the core of *The Wings of the Dove.* Maggie Verver, the daughter of a fabulously wealthy American widower in England, discovers that her husband, the Roman prince Amerigo, has an adulterous liaison with Charlotte Stant, a childhood friend of hers. The affair is doubly adulterous since Charlotte has become the second wife of Maggie's father, Adam Verver. The cast includes most of the major types of James's international dramas: the innocent American girl, the wealthy but bland and tolerant American father, the European nobleman, as well as two types of American expatriates. Charlotte Stant, for one, is pointedly reminiscent of Gilbert Osmond of *The Portrait of a Lady,* in fact, might almost be his daughter: born in Florence, her parents American but "already of a corrupt generation, demoralized falsified polyglot well before her," herself—like Pansy Osmond—schooled in a Tuscan convent. The other expatriate type is represented by Fanny Assingham, the American wife of a British colonel, also a habitué of Europe and reminiscent of Maria Gostrey of *The Ambassadors* not merely because, like her, she functions as a *ficelle* but because her particular role imposes on her a similar passion for supersubtle hunches. In Fanny Assingham the role is pushed to ironic extremes. She is a caricature of the Jamesian clair-voyante, and the final absurdities of her lucidity, always pointed up by the placid common sense of her soothingly unimaginative husband, have a minor thematic significance.

But despite these traditional features, *The Golden Bowl* is among the most emblematic of James's novels. More than most others it is removed from what is called the stuff of ordinary life, and it caters less than most to the reader's pleasure of recognition. For *The Golden Bowl* is not a realistic novel in the ordinary sense of the term. It is a fable whose very subject is the interaction of two different attitudes toward the same events. The drama, though of breathless suspense, is all internal, all—as James says in the preface—"subject to the register, ever so closely kept, of the consciousness" of the two major characters. The very structure derives from the conflict between their two points of view, from the interplay of the Prince's experience of Maggie and her experience of him. For, to quote the preface once more, in the first volume the Prince "opens the door to half our light upon Maggie," just as in the second volume she "opens it to half our light upon himself; the rest of our impression, in either case, coming straight from the very motion with which that act is performed."[2] Even most of the other characters appear to us only as first the Prince and later Maggie apprehend them. What we are thus given to see is the gradual convergence of their originally divergent points of view, a process which is externalized by the transformation of their marriage.

The marriage itself is emblematic. It begins as a marriage of American wealth to European nobility, motivated on the European side by the need to make nobility solvent, on the American side by the desire to appropriate the tangible signs of tradition and age. Both these motivations are clearly established early in the novel when the Prince remembers one of his early conversations with Maggie. Quite naïvely she has told him that he is part of her father's collection of treasures, "a rarity, an object of beauty, an object of price," and he has remembered the high price which Mr. Verver has had to pay for him. But of the price Maggie knows nothing. Her ingenuous rendering of her father's view has been possible only because that view is wholly extraneous to her own, to her love for the Prince. All of which he recognizes: Maggie is "not of this age" of bargains between American billionaires and impoverished European noblemen; a "braver and finer" age, even his own cinquecento, would not have been ashamed of her as it would be of him. Yet, though he recognizes all this, though he is charmed by her, he is not moved. The marriage, in spite of Maggie, begins as a marriage of convenience, and it is this marriage of convenience which the Prince does not regard as being a sacred bond.

In turn, however, the freedom of his affair with Charlotte Stant works a change in Maggie. By her discovery of what has happened she is jolted out of her complacent girlish innocence. She becomes lucid and thereby capable of her native strength. She comes to see the causes of her failure: that her tender concern for her father has not only kept her from being a wife, but has represented her as acquiescing in all innocence in his conventional view of her marriage; that Amerigo in effect has *been* a mere *morceau de musée;* that in her blindness she has fostered this view of his role. What she makes of this knowledge, and what it makes of her, enables her to handle the situation in such a manner as to convince the Prince of her own substance, not as the charming little daughter of a romantic American millionaire, but as an intelligent and passionate woman. So that the end finds their marriage transmuted into a passionate union.

On one level, then, *The Golden Bowl* is a fable emblematic of the achievement of the international "social fusion" which James envisioned as the ultimate result of the increasingly intimate social relations between Europe and America.[3] And to say that an "inevitably futile existence"[4] is awaiting them is no more relevant to Maggie and Amerigo than it would be to any fairy princess and prince condemned to live happily ever after. For the focus of the fable is not sociological but moral. Nor, surely, is it doing justice to Maggie to maintain that "since she keeps her innocence intact," the knowledge which she gets of evil is "unnatural," that she "has her cake and eats it too."[5] The point is not so much that by her own suffering she has heavily paid for her knowledge; it is above all that part of her knowledge is of her own innocent complicity, for she learns that her own ignorance, that other side of the coin of innocence, has been a necessary condition of the evil which to her horror she comes to find "seated all at its ease" where she has "dreamed only of good." Her tender relation with her father has been part of that innocence, and the crucial result of her new wisdom, the sign also of its great personal cost to her, is the fact that at the end she accepts her separation from him, realizing that she can indeed *not* have the cake and eat it too, that if her marriage is to be the emotional reality which alone will compel the Prince, she must give up the father who has conceived it as the mere acquisition of another treasure.

It is important to understand Adam Verver and the role he plays in the international theme of the novel. He is a puzzling figure, but his role and the whole novel become clearer as soon as we cease to assume, as recent critcis seem to have assumed, that James intended to present him in a wholly sympathetic light, that he was blind to Adam Verver's warped view of fundamental values.[6] Such assumptions are unwarranted, for Adam Verver is part of Maggie's immaturity and represents a stage in the American relation to Europe which must be purged before the intimate "social fusion" symbolized by her final understanding with the Prince is possible.

There are, in the first place, plenty of indications of James's critical detachment from the "little man," plenty of passages whose irony, though perhaps too subtly subdued, nevertheless cuts deep. Take Mr. Verver's scheme for American City, the master plan of his whole career as a collector. After a highly successful business career Adam Verver has had a sudden revelation; he has realized that he has in him "the spirit of the connoisseur." And from this point of exaltation, from his "peak in Darien"—for James ironically presents him as seeing himself under the image of Keats's stout Cortez—he has conceived for himself the mission of bringing to the "thirsty millions" of his native state beyond the Mississippi the high knowledge of art. He feels himself "equal somehow with the great seers, the invokers and encouragers of beauty" and not after all "so far below the great producers and creators" themselves. And since the years of his benightedness before the vital revelation luckily brought him a fortune wholly equal to the height of his new exaltation, his mission can take the form of a "museum of museums, a palace of art" which is to be "compact as a Greek temple was compact, a receptacle of treasures sifted to positive sanctity," as a gift to his fellow-citizens designed to meet fully the "urgency" of their "release from the bondage of ugliness." All this comes to us in the terms in which Amerigo remembers Mr. Verver expressing his own conception, and the pointed solemnity of the language contains more than a grain of irony. For surely we are not to think of James as envisaging the wholesale abduction of European art and its monumental installation in a western American City as the "ideal program" for retired tycoons devoting themselves to the charitable dispensation of culture! The idea is so at odds with one's sense of what James stood for that it is almost embarrassing to have to argue its absurdity. But one remembers other such portraits in James's gallery, portraits showing a family likeness to Adam Verver, though less subtly drawn and therefore less easily misunderstood.

There is, for instance, the pompous Mr. Leavenworth of *Roderick Hudson,* "lately retired from the proprietorship of large mines of borax in the Middle West" and now in Europe collecting "memorials" for his "large residential structure" on the Ohio, where with their help he hopes "to recover a certain degree of tone," his pet project being the "library, filled with well-selected and beautifully-bound authors in groups relieved from point to point by high-class statuary." One also remembers Christopher Newman's order to Mademoiselle Noémie to copy for him all the *largest* canvases of the Louvre, price being no matter. Above all, however, one thinks of Mr. Bender in *The Outcry* (1910-11), the American collector most closely approaching Adam Verver as far as the scale of his operations is concerned. Mr. Bender is after expensive pictures; whether they are good is of little importance to him as long as the prices are sensational. What makes this parallel particularly suggestive is the fact that the very subject of *The Outcry* is the denudation of English country houses by American collectors. And though James's condemnation here falls most heavily on the irresponsible cupidity of the British owners, the story leaves no doubt what he thought of the cultural value of the helter-skelter transportation of art treasures across the Atlantic or of the moral influence of American wealth on impoverished aristocrats. And when, returning to *The Golden Bowl*, we read that Mr. Verver hopes from another couple of years in Europe a "refreshed sensibility to the currents of the market," that he cares "that a work of art should 'look like' the master to whom it might perhaps be deceitfully attributed," despite the ambiguity of the last sentence, we gather under the spell of the immediate context the suggestion of something not unlike Mr. Bender's carelessness of authenticity.

At any rate, under the subdued appeals scattered throughout the extended passage which acquaints us with Adam Verver's background, our sense of the tenuousness of his values wakes up more and more. And when we hear of his belief that his cultural mission retroactively justifies "the livid vulgarity" of his early years in the service of mammon, his belief that a "wiser hand than he at first knew had kept him hard at acquisition of one sort as a perfect preliminary to acquisition of another," James's irony should escape us no longer. In his search for *objets d'art* Adam Verver has "ceased on the whole to know any matter of the rest of life by its looks." Not only his view of Maggie's marriage, but his own to Charlotte Stant, too, is symptomatic. The "great little man's" bedazzlement is generic and part of James's intention.

If all this can escape us sometimes, the reason is simply that we see Mr. Verver almost entirely in reflection, primarily in the minds of the Prince and Maggie. They, however, never express themselves openly about him. It is not so much that Maggie is too tender a daughter to be critical of her father, nor that she is too loyal to express whatever criticism she may come to think, though both facts do in turn act as a restraint. The main reason of their reticence, Maggie's and the Prince's, is something which bears directly on the moral theme of the novel so that the very difficulty which the reader experiences in assessing Mr. Verver's character is part of James's intended effect. What must be kept in mind is the fact that the subject of the novel is the gradual coalescence of Maggie's and the Prince's moral consciousness. And their silence about their attitudes toward Mr. Verver is part of what finally constitutes their common moral code.

The theme of the moral contrast is struck at the very beginning of the novel. Even before his marriage, Amerigo is afraid "of being 'off' some day, of being wrong, *without* knowing it"; for the knowledge of being wrong, the moral sense as Americans understand it, is something which, he feels, he lacks. To be sure, he has something that in "poor dear backward old Rome sufficiently passes for it," but to the American sense of such matters it compares as does the crumbling stone staircase of a *quattrocento* castle to the "lightning elevator" of an American skyscraper. "Your moral sense," he tells his American confidante, "works by steam—it sends you up like a rocket. Ours is slow and steep and unlighted, with so many of the steps missing that—well, that it's as short in almost any case to turn round and come down again." The last image suggests the same contrast as in the first two novels of the trilogy: between the exaltations of absolute idealism and an ethical tradition which is the cumulative product of historical experience whose validity is measured by the test of workability.

What we have just seen is Amerigo's sense of the matter; but something similar is felt on the other side when, telling the Prince that he is "inveterately round," a "pure and perfect crystal," Mr. Verver expresses his grateful sense of the ease of daily intercourse made possible by Amerigo's high polish. But Amerigo sees further; he realizes that some crystals "have cracks and flaws," just as earlier he has realized that some of the steps of his old moral staircase are missing so that it may not serve in all contingencies. He is aware of the chasm hidden by the superficial agreement, aware how often the Ververs misconceive him; and not having an analytical mind, he can only fall back on "his general explanation—'we haven't the same values,'" which is of course what his relation to Charlotte, now Mrs. Verver, illustrates. For in his affair with her he is indeed at first not conscious of "being wrong." Maggie seems absorbed only in her father; and Charlotte, thrust upon him by father and daughter in their "pathetic simplicity and good faith,"[7] is there before him in her brilliant splendor, beautiful and aggressive, and to refuse her expert addresses would seem "to publish one as idiotic or incapable." The situation, the "essential opposition of theories," strikes him as positively grotesque—"as if a galantuomo, as *he* at least constitutionally conceived galantuomini, could do anything *but* blush to 'go about' at such a rate with such a person as Mrs. Verver in a state of childlike innocence." Moreover, "we're happy —and they're happy. What more does the position admit of?"— thus, in his lighter moments, he can pragmatize, reducing the ethics of the situation to a question of discretion and tact.

It is, however, precisely here that Amerigo is distinguished from Charlotte. To accept the situation created by the intimacy of father and daughter as long as they can be kept safe from the knowledge which would destroy their innocent peace seems to him the only way of meeting his predicament, since he realizes more and more how little he has in him of the "general tradition," of the "moral paste" of the Ververs. Charlotte, on the other hand, is "of the same race." If Amerigo's lack of sharp corners, as Mr. Verver has put it to him, and the ease, too, of his moral accommodations are the result of long social experience, what *seems* the same social expertness in Charlotte is really a wholly different matter—the result not of a slow and perhaps incomplete growth but of a recent corruption. The same conduct, or what appears to be the same conduct, has different foundations in him and her; the same appearances hide realities different because they are conditioned by different civilizations. To draw once more on *The Portrait of a Lady,* this difference forms a parallel to the difference between Warburton and Osmond, who constitute similar threats to Isabel Archer's moral existence, but whose different antecedents nevertheless give them motives of wholly dissimilar moral values. The difference between Amerigo and Charlotte, too, is that his tact, although it serves to cover his own freedom, is motivated very largely by an alert sense of social responsibility, a sense of the needs of others, hers by a sense of her own needs.

The difference is marked by a multitude of hints and touches, beginning in what is one of the most amazing scenes in all of James—the scene in which Charlotte and Amerigo acknowledge their full awareness of the situation created for them by the mutual absorption of the Ververs. Charlotte and Amerigo are literally abandoned to each other, and the scene ends in their common assertion that the Ververs' innocent simplicity must be their constant "sacred" care. But when they seal this pledge with their first passionate embrace, the reader is likely to gasp at what seems a perversion of moral feeling almost blasphemous, all the more because it is not designed to deceive anybody but themselves. Already, however, Charlotte is the more suspect of the two. She insists on their own helplessness:

Nothing stranger surely had ever happened to a conscientious, a well-meaning, a perfectly passive pair: no more extraordinary decree had ever been launched against such victims than this of forcing them against their will into a relation of mutual close contact that they had done everything to avoid.

Her hypocrisy, immediately recognized by Amerigo, is the sign of her fall from a higher knowledge. Amerigo, in his greater moral simplicity, on the other hand, is neither in need nor capable of hypocrisy. One is reminded of James's remark in the *Notebooks* that "hiding and lying" make English adultery "so much more ugly" than French. For what distinguishes Charlotte essentially from Amerigo is that, in order to achieve her will, she can violate a conscience in her already weakened by corruption, in him not yet fully awake.

Indeed, almost as soon as their compact is made, the falsity of his position arouses in him an unrest, an irritation fed by "the red spark of his inextinguishable sense of a higher and braver propriety"

—feelings to which Charlotte in her cold selfishness is immune. The difference becomes a question of candor, the quality so central in James's moral thinking: Amerigo can shudder at the thought that Fanny Assingham, for instance, might let him see that she does not trust him; Charlotte, to his surprise, should not mind since Fanny can do them no harm. Safety in their clandestine affair to him means more than anything else the Ververs' safety from painful knowledge; to Charlotte it means the freedom of their own pursuit of pleasure. All of which and all of what follows throws a backward light on their passionate pledge: he has stood in wonderment before what to him is the abysmal innocence of the Ververs; she has rejoiced in it as the source of their ease; and though their words, his "it's sacred," which she has readily echoed—are the same, their meaning, their motives are not.

What follows proves this. For almost as soon as the edge of their desire is dulled, as soon as their elation abates under the sobering impact of their established freedom, the difference between them turns into a rift. Amerigo has unconsciously forecast it when in answer to her assertion that he is at any rate not "too different" from her, he has said, "I don't know—as we're not married"; perhaps if they were, she *"would* find some abyss of divergence." Though, to be sure, they are not married, now the common course of their lives is subject to regularity and routine as if they were. And his interest, which she has first appealed to through her splendor, through a talent for the "great life" much like Kate Croy's of *The Wings of the Dove,* now, much like Densher's interest, is gradually superseded by a greater. Maggie's voice comes to have a new tone; Maggie has surprises for him, depths not suspected before, has reserves of power —all of which Charlotte, all her hard splendor on daily display, lacks, so that her hold on Amerigo slackens and he, finally, not so much returns to Maggie, the girl, as for the first time takes possession of the woman.

What finally unites him and Maggie is the mutual experience of each other which has been needed to make their moral education complete. Maggie, after first sensing, then clearly seeing, the flaw in the chalice of her marriage, with a movement reminiscent of Densher's eluding of Kate Croy's arms, has refused to be possessed by Amerigo until she fully possesses him. This refusal is her first act of personal existence; in it she casts off the role which Amerigo and her father, in staging the conventional play, have cast her in—the role of the innocent American girl marrying her wealth to European nobility. Her physical withdrawal, motivated psychologically, is a symbol of her emancipation from a view in which Adam Verver is no less implicated than the Prince has been. But it is part of her new mastery of life that nothing indicates the severing of her accord with her father—nothing except that in finally abandoning him to American City and his collection, she repudiates, without the passing of a single word, the relation with him which has been the sign of her immaturity.

The last two scenes of the book—the first between Maggie and her father, who still speaks in the lingo of the collector, the second between her and Amerigo—are charged with this, though all but the final liberation of Maggie's and Amerigo's mutual and private love is veiled in irony. But we are not to suppose that Maggie's freedom is the result of easy ingratitude. The knowledge which has made her humanity complete is that there is no life without pain, no life without painful choices, and her choice between father and husband once more proves it. Nor are good and evil comfortably apportioned. James did not, as has been blithely assumed,[8] intend Charlotte and the Prince as "the only wrongdoers," nor did he withhold from Charlotte all "pathetic or tragic sympathy." Maggie, whose consciousness dominates the whole of the second volume, can think of Charlotte as "a soul in pain," can be moved to tears by the quaver of anguish in her high, hard voice. And one of her last comments on all that has happened—"It's always terrible for women"—is spoken with Charlotte above all in mind, Charlotte who has lost the Prince and is doomed to presiding over Mr. Verver's treasures in American City. Maggie's sympathy with Charlotte is subtly marked by contrast with Amerigo's greater detachment: "Everything's terrible, cara—in the heart of man. She's making her life," he says. "A little by the way then too, while she's about it, she's making ours," Maggie answers, for she knows that without Charlotte's threat to their peace she herself might still be Mr. Verver's little girl and therefore might not possess the Prince as she now does.

Maggie's comprehension has indeed "soared" high—not exactly to a transcendental trust in the beneficence of evil, for James's Americanism had much more of Hawthorne than of Emerson, but to the realization of how subtly intertwined the good and the evil can be. The image dominating the critical scene in which her new knowledge almost overcomes her suggests this clearly: her father and her husband with Charlotte and Fanny Assingham are seated around the bridge table; "the facts of the situation" are "upright for her around the green cloth and the silver flambeaux; the fact of her father's wife's lover facing his mistress; the fact of her father sitting, all unsounded and unblinking, between them; the fact of Charlotte keeping it up, keeping up everything, across the table, with her husband beside her; the fact of Fanny Assingham" sitting opposite the three and "knowing more about each" than "either of them knew of either. Erect above all for her" is "the sharp-edged fact of the relation of the whole group, individually and collectively, to herself —herself so speciously eliminated for the hour, but presumably more present to the attention of each than the next card to be played." It is this symbolic picture of the "apparently straight play" which strikes her with "the horror of the thing hideously *behind,* behind so much trusted, so much pretended, nobleness, cleverness, tenderness." To her sense, they are all alike implicated in this "first sharp falsity" in her life, and her father quite specifically is a "high adept, one of the greatest," at the symbolic game. Her horrified sense of finding "evil seated all at its ease" where she has "only dreamed of good" is no mere matter of Charlotte's treachery, for Maggie knows that Charlotte, too, is a victim, child that she is of parents already uprooted and corrupt, and now betrayed into a marriage sterile in all but the glamour of material well-being.

But *The Golden Bowl* is not primarily Charlotte's story. The focus on the consciousness of Amerigo and Maggie makes it theirs, makes it the story of a struggle, except in its outcome and its much deeper moral search, not wholly unlike that of Bessie Alden and Lord Lambeth of "An International Episode" against the web of convention. The triumph is theirs, Maggie's primarily, but Amerigo's too. It is at any rate not the triumph of America over Europe. Rather it is the triumphant complementing of one by the other. For if Amerigo is moved by Maggie's virtue, what so compels him is not only her love but also that other, older excellence contained in the word—the fortitude and potent discipline with which she meets her crisis.

Once Maggie has stepped beyond the walls of her cloistered childhood, she finds herself on the brink of an abyss of sordid disorder, in Stephen Spender's words, "of the divorce court, the reported evidence of servants, and love-letters printed in the news."[9] The sense of the injustice done to her is a grave temptation for her to cry out, to take "the straight vindictive view," to exercise "the rights of resentment." But it is a temptation overcome almost as soon as felt, and the rich imagery with which James conveys the growth of Maggie's lucidity rings with an authenticity which puts its crucial significance beyond doubt. Because of the threat of destruction and chaos inherent in them, the "protests of passion" figure to Maggie "nothing nearer to experience than a wild eastern caravan, looming into view with crude colors in the sun, fierce pipes in the air, high spears against the sky," all a thrill of release, "but turning off short" before reaching her "and plunging into other defiles." She realizes that to destroy "the beauty of appearances" still so perfectly preserved not only would gain her nothing but would amount to her giving up whatever still ties her to the partners of her life. And so she ends by taking her knowledge upon her to bear alone, to the extent of assuring Charlotte, when challenged, that she has never thought of her "but as beautiful, wonderful and good." "Upon your honour?" "Upon my honour," Maggie replies. And the scene ends with a Gethsemane which freezes the extraordinary inversion of the right and wrong of falsehood and truth: "Will you kiss me on it then?" Charlotte demands. But the most Maggie can do is to suffer Charlotte's kiss, the kiss which completes "the coldness of their conscious perjury."

Maggie has stopped short of the archetypal act of betrayal, yet she has lied. If the reader flounders in ambiguity, this is part of James's intention, part of his thematic concern with the conflict between absolute and pragmatic morality. Maggie's lie is part of her denying herself the cry for justice. She has seen her choice not between what is true, what false, not between what is pure, what impure, but as determined by what the given conditions seem to make right. She has seen it as a choice of peopling the scene of her life "either with serenities and dignities and decencies, or with terrors and shames and ruins," and she has chosen the first, feeling that since the unruffled surface indicates so much "firm ground" still between them all, the deformity is all in her own attitude. Of this her lie is the correction. From the point of view of simple moral absolutism, this looks of course like "spiritual legerdemain,"[10] but to dramatize the limitations of moral absolutism as a guide to conduct is part of James's intention. As in *The Ambassadors*, this significance of the lie is emphasized beyond mistake: James spares Maggie no awareness of what she is doing. "The right," she sees, takes "this extraordinary form of humbugging" to the end; it is "a question of not by a hair's breadth deflecting into the truth." And in her very abasement before Charlotte, she can feel her heart swell with a proud sense of keeping "in tune with the right."

Yet the shocking inversion of values is not of her doing. Her motive is to preserve her marriage, her means are determined by the web of deceit in which her life is caught. Her method has almost something of the psychiatric since, far from forcing Amerigo to renounce a real passion, she makes him avail himself of her lucidity and thus leads him to an awareness of the cursory nature of his involvement with Charlotte. The sureness with which she proceeds once the moment of her weakness, the temptation of despair is past, constitutes for Amerigo a revelation not unlike the one which Milly Theale brings to Densher. This is the emphatic note on which the book closes: "I see nothing but *you*," Amerigo tells her, and the light in his eyes proclaims "the truth of it." For Maggie has aroused him to the first passion equal to the depth of feeling he is capable of.

What Amerigo sees is the profundity of Maggie's own passion, for this too is part of her awakening. This too, above all, is the source of her self-discipline, since not to give up the partners of her life means in effect not to give up her husband. What has impelled her is the desire for the constancy without which life is chaos. And it is part of her maturity that she is capable of shouldering the burden of moral ambiguity which is inseparable from living. If the last wisdom which Marie de Vionnet of *The Ambassadors* learns is that taking does not assure happiness, that "the only safe thing is to give," if in giving Milly Theale of *The Wings of the Dove* finds a means to the fulness of life otherwise denied her—the wisdom which Maggie acts upon, though it brushes these, is sadder. Her story, with its suggestion of the inevitability, not merely of feeling pain, but of inflicting it, is in a sense more tragic than the tragedy of Milly. For Maggie, since she is not subjected to the last agony Milly has to endure, is not granted the opportunity for transfiguration either. Yet, if the happiness she wins falls short of beatitude, it is only because she has so admirably learned how to meet life.

She is fully conscious of the cost of her own fulness of life, not only to Charlotte, but also to her father. She can live her own life, she can be wife, only by breaking the bond which has tied her so wholly to him that it has been the starting point of a vicious circle in which the devotion of father and daughter and the intimacy of their *sposi* have mutually impelled each other. Maggie can break out of this because she has outgrown the "pathetic simplicity" of her childhood. But she must sacrifice the object of her childish devotion. Significantly, her realization of this need follows immediately upon the scene of her equally necessary perjury. Her climactic meeting with Charlotte is followed by a conversation with her father in which she feels him mutely pressing upon her "a sacrifice" which she mutely accepts: he will take himself and Charlotte out of her life to American City. That Adam Verver has been able to recognize this as "her best possibility" is a sign that his vision, too, has grown, though too late for his own salvation: for him nothing is left but to act out his role and to take Charlotte with him to the limbo of those whom an earlier time has placed in a false relation to Europe. There is a certain cruelty involved in this, but it is the cruelty of Nemesis. Maggie, at worst, is its instrument, and unless we are prepared to demand that she acquiesce in bearing sins not her own, we must admire her for taking her life in her own hands.

But *The Golden Bowl* is the story also of Amerigo's growth—though, since the second volume focuses entirely on Maggie's consciousness, it is traced much less fully than hers. Nevertheless, the difference between the early Amerigo and the late is striking. The early Amerigo is irresponsible with the charming irresponsibility of a child. The fairy world of romantic innocence and literally fabulous wealth to which his alliance with the Ververs has admitted him strikes him with wide-eyed and guileless wonder. For all his urbane knowingness is of surfaces alone—though, to be sure, surfaces serving honorably as far as surfaces go. Hence the benevolent amusement with which he accepts the role which the Ververs have assigned him in their play at international marriage. Ease is perhaps what characterizes him most. Even his temporary abandonment to the appeal of Charlotte's beauty and expert address, ecstatic as it is, lacks the depth which would make it problematic to him. In his first preliminary note for *The Golden Bowl,* more than ten years before the book was published, James envisaged the young husband as "clever, various, inconstant, amiable, cynical, unscrupulous—charming always, to 'the other woman' "; and though the editors of the *Notebooks* are right when they comment that Amerigo "is of firmer moral fiber,"[11] in the early parts of the novel this firmer moral fiber is largely dormant. The early Amerigo is in fact less weighty than James's first conception of him, because his consciousness as yet lacks everything to which a moral value can well be attached: though he is clever, amiable, always charming—and by no means only to the "other woman"—he is neither cynical nor unscrupulous, nor, for that matter, inconstant, and all quite simply because he has as yet no moral awareness to betray, no real attachment to forsake. Despite his polish he is, in fact, not unlike Hawthorne's Donatello of the furry ears, something of an Arcadian character. Or he is an older version of those relatively "formed" European children James knew in his boyhood and remembered in *A Small Boy and Others* as "the trained and admonished, the disciplined and governessed," aware of "many things," yet with an awareness which struck him even then as "at the best imperfect."[12]

Something of this ease may seem to remain with Amerigo to the end since, in spite of his awakening, he makes no positive acknowledgment of past fault. Should he have shown her "a little more handsomely" that he accepts her knowledge of the crack in the golden bowl of their marriage, he asks Maggie? And when she says that it is not a question of beauty but of good faith, all he can answer is, "If ever a man since the beginning of time acted in good faith—!" One might suspect him of prevarication were it not that his conduct proves his truth. His good faith was the good faith of the unmoral child. That is why what he finally acknowledges is not his past fault, but his new awareness of what Maggie has done for him. The proof he offers is, significantly, not something done, not something said, but something left unsaid: he has kept his knowledge of her knowledge secret from Charlotte, demonstrating thus his changed allegiance. But for the final proof, the positive testimony of his surrender, he asks Maggie to wait till Charlotte and Adam Verver have left them—"for as long as God may grant! Till we're really alone."

The reason for Amerigo's passivity is that Maggie is the one who guides and rules their relationship and the moral awakening it involves for him. She combines in one person the roles which in *The Wings of the Dove* are divided between Milly and the all-wise Sir Luke. As long as the world represented by the others is still with them, she treats him in fact somewhat like a parent responsible for the education, though meticulously considerate of the dignity and self-respect, of a child. Such paternalism might strike the reader as unpleasant were it not that Maggie has subjected herself to the even harder discipline required of her role; were it not, above all, that when they finally are alone, everything drops from her except her devotion, in which giving and taking are one.

The passionate harmony of their final union, pointedly set off against the precariously sustained harmony of their last meeting with Adam Verver and Charlotte, is on one level the symbol of the meeting of America and Europe, the concrete image of the "idea of some eventual sublime consensus" which James, as he wrote in one of the prefaces, had from far back seen lurking "behind all the small comedies and tragedies of the international."[13] Adam and Charlotte both appropriate the superficies of European form, the one for purposes of exportation and exhibition, the other as a convenient cover for dimly felt license. Such attitudes as theirs were the stuff of those "small comedies and tragedies" and had to be eliminated before a real "fusion" was possible—if it is ever possible. For just as the subject of *The Golden Bowl* reaches far beyond the international situation, so the closing scene represents more than a social fusion. It is in fact a symbolic climax of the mutual interfusion of two virtues—of the discipline of Maggie's spiritual energy by Amerigo's form, the quickening penetration of his form by her spirit—possible only to the high intelligence on which their love is based.[14] And if it represents a "sublime consensus," it is not merely the consensus of "the educated" James was looking forward to; it is a consensus of the good which remains one of man's needs.

VII
The Expatriate As American

ALMOST from the moment when James began to live abroad, his relations to America and Europe began to be misunderstood. The English regarded "An International Episode" as a piece of impudence, the Americans "Daisy Miller" as an outrage upon American girlhood. In America his expatriation led to a lusty growth of opinion, fervent and ingenious rather than sound, of which the theories of Parrington and Van Wyck Brooks are the most eminent examples.[1] At times American resentment of James's defection was no more than the product of nationalistic or social dogmatism miffed by James's detachment. At others it was more respectable: an expression of that literary nationalism which had sprung from the need of transforming a colonial culture into a domestic one. The revolt against cultural dependence on Europe, voiced most impressively perhaps by Emerson but sooner or later voiced also by many others, demanded that American writers deal with American themes. But often this prescription was simplified; they were to celebrate the American scene, narrowly understood. Yet there are several Americas, and settings need not indicate much about an author's point of view. Hawthorne, for instance, is just as American, though he may not be so good an artist, in *The Marble Faun* as he is in *The Scarlet Letter*. And James is American, and never more profoundly so than in his late novels, for only an American could have portrayed Americans as he did.

Europeans perhaps see this more easily than Americans do. European critics, at any rate, saw it early. M. S. Gretton, an Englishman, said in 1912 that James's vision had remained thoroughly "trans-Atlantic"; in 1891 a French critic pointed to James's "américanisme robuste, vivace, persistant" as the principal interest in his works.[2] T. S. Eliot spoke of the same thing, though from a different point of view, when he said that only an American could *"properly* appreciate James." Indeed it is doubtful that Europeans respond "properly" to James's portraits of the American in Europe, for, although they may have brushed against him, wined and dined him, not many are likely to have penetrated to the sources of his being. If, as James had to remind the readers of *The Nation* in 1878, Americans in Europe remained outsiders,[3] the reverse was similarly true. Few Europeans were at home in the second American colonies, the colonies in Europe. Few had been to the "Europe" of the American imagination since—this was the meaning of James's essay in the *Nation*—their homes and "our old home" were not the same thing. Whoever had heard of a good Englishman, German, Italian— or even Frenchman—going to Paris to die?

Yet, if James's point of view remained in important respects American, he was like many good Americans an Anglophile. But he could afford to criticize where he loved. Thanks to his unique opportunities, the American desire for Europe was in him so thoroughly fulfilled that no hankering and therefore no secondary resentment remained. His eclectic education had accomplished the purpose for which it had been designed: by loosening local attachments, it had prepared him for citizenship in a country transcending national boundaries. This is why from the very first the English too could strike him as provincial—why in 1877, for instance, he could write to one of his friends that, "thanks to that combination of the continent and the U.S.A." which had formed his lot, he found himself "a good deal more of a cosmopolitan" than the average cultivated Englishman.[4] His cosmopolitanism was an "accident," the "uncomfortable consequence of seeing many lands and feeling at home in none."[5] Thus he put it in an essay of 1878 later included in *Portraits of Places*. And early stories like "An International Episode" exemplify his detachment from the British and American points of view alike, though also his sympathetic understanding of both. Much later, Hamlin Garland and Amy Lowell were to report that he seemed to regret his dislocation, and his tribute to Howells' seventy-fifth birthday reads almost like a public confession of such regrets.[6] Just how serious they were is of course difficult to know, but they too suggest that to have become an expatriate apparently was neither to have been anglicized nor to have ceased being an American.

Cosmopolitanism had been imposed upon James by his upbringing, and as an artist he exploited what as a man he could not help. Any further diagnosis of his case has to take into account the different values which the two worlds separated by the Atlantic represented for him. And if the all but continuous adumbration of a moral bias in favor of America contained in his international fiction suggests that, despite his expatriation, the sources of his inspiration remained in the country of his birth, it is possible to show in addition that the very foundations even of his cosmopolitanism were inherent in his American consciousness.

James's final naturalization as a British subject in 1915 serves as a convenient starting point. This step, taken only a few months before his death, was given something of the character of a public demonstration by the fact that one of James's sponsors was the British Prime Minister. In part for this reason, it has sometimes been taken as the culmination of his alienation from America. But this is to misunderstand his motives. And since his change of citizenship was indeed a symbolical act, the meaning James himself saw in it provides a key to his complex relations to America and England.

The crux lies in an apparent ambiguity of James's own statements about the matter. In his letters he says several times that,
without the war, he would have remained what he was—an American citizen living in England. A few hours after taking the oath of
allegiance, on the other hand, he wrote that naturalization had
merely shown him what he already "virtually *was*."[7] But if we
remember his unpolitical nature, if we remember above all the
childhood filled with the crossing of frontiers in search of education,
the contradiction resolves itself quite simply. To a world so charged
with the fear of subversion that it regards loyalty as a matter of
political allegiance pure and simple the fact may seem strange, but
the declaration of loyalty to England did not to James's mind
involve an abrogation of his loyalty to the United States. From the
beginning of the war, he had waited for American intervention. His
letters of these months testify to the fervor of a participation which
eloquently denies the theory of his remoteness from life. Above all,
they show how with the continuation of official American neutrality
he came to feel more and more that the attitude of the government
in Washington misrepresented his own. His sense of being an
"outsider to the whole situation here," as he says in one letter,
became acute when he found that as an American citizen he could
travel between London and Rye only "on the footing of an Alien
under Police supervision."[8] But this does not mean that, as has been
suggested,[9] his motive for becoming naturalized was simple convenience. As the particular letter indicates, these restrictions served
primarily to point up for him the incongruity of his official position
as a neutral American. And his sense of the falseness of this position
finally became so irksome to him that he was moved to demonstrate
his belief in the British cause by a formal declaration which, as he
said, was to show America "a little something of the way."[10] For
while Washington dawdled, James was sure what that way would
ultimately be. And if the independence of his course of action in
1915 was politically unorthodox, the events of 1917 justified his
motives at least.

James's position can be reduced to two principles to which American history easily supplies parallels. For one thing, his first allegiance was not to a state—whether England or America—but to a cause, which he considered the cause of civilization. Apart from the meticulous legality of his procedure, his break with his government was not unlike Thoreau's civil disobedience, for instance, both springing from a sense of the sovereignty of the individual conscience. And during the Great War itself—as again during World War II before Pearl Harbor—a sympathy with the Allied cause similar to James's led the younger Americans of the ambulance corps to break the official neutrality of their government. Such physical participation was impossible for James, though he could and did support the American volunteers with the weight of his written word. What he could further do, after vainly waiting a full year for a change in the official American attitude, was to throw whatever moral weight his example might have into the scales on the Allied side. Underlying his sense of the justice of the Allied cause, moreover—just as it had been underlying Mark Twain's attitude in the Boer War—was a sense of kinship between America and England. If James's differed from Mark Twain's, it did so primarily by its unpolitical orientation, since his sense of cultural ties had always been stronger than his sense of political frontiers. His letters show that he became more and more certain of the gradual awakening of what he called the "American identity of consciousness"[11] with England at war. And the resolution of whatever may appear paradoxical in the attitude externalized by his naturalization is to be found, not in any change of *his* relations to the two countries, but in his sense of *their* relation to each other.

James's sense of the unity of the Anglo-Saxon world was, however, no mere fruit of the war. As early as 1888, he had written to William that he could not "look at the English-American world" save as "a big Anglo-Saxon total," destined to melt together more and more. His "Anglo-Saxonism"—the term is his own—goes back still farther, at least as far as the travel essays of 1876 and 1878.

Naturally when he first settled in London in 1876, he was conscious of Anglo-American differences. But after months of immersion in English society, after the ordeal of dining out "107 times" in one season, which he reports in a letter of 1879, his interest in the contrast between American and English manners understandably flagged. Much later Edith Wharton was to recall the change which came over him after he had "taken the measure" of fashionable society. The fastidious *"homme du monde* of the eighties" developed into the imposing figure of "voluminous outline" and sculptured Roman head. The beard gave way to the clean shave revealing the "big dramatic mouth"—all tokens to her of the emancipation of his genius. It was part of this emancipation that he now gradually turned from the conflict of manners to deeper probings into human conduct, probings which demanded the finer distinctions of a world of unified conventions. Hence his turn to purely English subjects. But hence, too, his growing interest in "Anglo-Saxonism." Increased intimacy with Europe had made him more aware of the differences between the European nations and, as a consequence, of the likenesses between American and English. "The *real* difference," he wrote to William in 1888, is "a gulf from the English (or the American) to the Frenchman and vice versâ" but "not from the Englishman to the American." Later he was to warn Edith Wharton against Franco-American subjects because the disparity between French and American life was too great to be useful to the novelist, was in fact as complete as between "monkeys and fish."[12]

The growth of his sense of the unity of the Anglo-Saxon character and its place in his later work is amusingly reflected in the *Notebooks,* where he worries repeatedly about the difficulty of presenting sexual irregularities to his readers—in 1887 to Americans, in 1888 to Anglo-Saxons, and in 1894 finally to the English.[13] Even when the relation between manners and morals became a central thematic concern of his fiction, the fear of offending English-speaking audiences continued to haunt him. In pondering the subject of *The Golden Bowl,* he felt his "fingers itch for it," as he put it in the *Notebooks* in 1895. *"Everything* about it qualifies it for *Harper* except . . . the adulterine element," but that, he told himself, might be "a question of *handling*," as indeed it turned out to be in that most Jamesian of all his novels. A similar problem is solved very much by handling in *The Wings of the Dove*. And the *Notebooks* passage (dated November, 1894) in which he works out the delicate relations between the characters who were to take shape as Kate Croy, Merton Densher, and Milly Theale, states his sense of the differences between French and Anglo-Saxon moral conventions with high clarity:

If I were writing for a French public the whole thing would be simple —the elder, the "other," woman [Kate Croy] would simply be the mistress of the young man [Densher], and it would be a question of his taking on the dying girl [Milly Theale] for a time—having a temporary liaison with her. But one can do so little with English adultery —it is so much less inevitable, and so much more ugly in all its hiding and lying side. It is so undermined by our immemorial tradition of original freedom of choice, and by our practically universal acceptance of divorce.

His shift from *American* to *English* as the designation of his own point of view has become complete. Not because he ceased to see differences between America and England, but because with regard to certain moral conventions the term *Anglo-Saxon* stood for a very real attitude. "Freedom of choice" had long before *The Wings of the Dove* been important in his portrayal of American girls, and Milly Theale herself finally emerged as one of them. But at the time of his preliminary ruminations he only *seemed* "to see her perhaps as an American." And similarly, in his first explorations of the *donnée* which developed into *The Ambassadors,* he noted in 1895 that Strether—though he has as yet no name—"may be an American— he might be an Englishman."

It is of course significant that in the end James saw Strether and Milly Theale as Americans. Their stories mark his return from purely English subjects to an internationalism in which the idea of

Anglo-Saxon unity, far as it may go to explain why he could make his life in England, plays less of a role than do contrasts between an American and another point of view which can only be called European.[14] No matter how real the affinity between America and England, the two nations were after all not identical. England had affinities with the European continent as well as with America, and the terms *European* and *Anglo-Saxon* each stood for a real communion in which she was embraced. Quite naturally James could be aware now more of one, now more of the other. Above all, he was so profoundly concerned with the American character and the moral qualities it represented for him, that other national characters came to serve him in the end primarily as a means of defining the uniqueness of the American. The question of morals, therefore, reattached itself to the question of the American character. The three great novels of his maturity—*The Ambassadors, The Wings of the Dove,* and *The Golden Bowl*—emerged as a trilogy dramatizing the relations of innocence and experience to morality in terms of conflicts between the American and the European conscience. And that at the height of his career James should find innocence and experience most readily juxtaposed wherever Americans and Europeans met, that Strether and Milly Theale, first conceived as English *or* American, should under the pressure of particular thematic needs end up as emphatically American—this in itself betrays the American bias of his moral view.

In the New York prefaces James states that the subjects of *The Wings of the Dove* and *The Golden Bowl* could have been expressed without recourse to an international cast of characters.[15] Why, then, did he nevertheless make these characters American, English, Italian? James's answer—for he anticipates the question—comes by way of a history of the "social relation" between America and Europe: what he called the "secondary" internationalism of his later fiction reflects in part simply his interest in the mixture of manners which resulted from the great increase of American travel to Europe. Around the turn of the century, he explains, the "monstrous" contrasts of the 1870's have begun to be attenuated in the closer "social fusion" of a new international society. And he forsees an eventual "consensus of the educated" whose dramatic possibilities will make the old "comedies and tragedies of the international" turn pale. As one follows his vision, one realizes that this future development is anticipated in the fusion of two different moral sensibilities which is the subject of *The Golden Bowl*. The contrast between that subtle novel, which ends in the union of an American girl and a Roman prince, and the short story of "Miss Gunton of Poughkeepsie," in which the union of another such pair goes on the rocks because the conflict of *their* manners is not attenuated by any "common intelligence"—this contrast illustrates the transformation of the international scene James had in mind.

It illustrates too the transformation of his own international fiction. His discussion of the question has begun with the assertion that human drama "subsists of course on contrast," and indeed, international contrast is at the basis of the novels of his maturity just as much as it is at the basis of his earlier stories. What has changed is his focus, what he calls his "subject." In the early stories, the conflict of manners *was* his subject; now it is merely his medium for the treatment of a moral subject which demands finer distinctions.[16] The days of *Transatlantic Sketches* and *Portraits of Places* or, as he says in a letter of 1903, of "little worthless, superficial, *poncif* articles"[17] about this place or that, are past—and the string of adjectives is a measure of what he now thinks of his old internationalism. In one of the prefaces he speaks of the "public" and "civic use" to which the imagination can be put "in the interest of morality." With such uses, the loud clash of manners can only interfere. In his late fiction, therefore, he has turned to the new polyglot world in which differences were rubbed off by familiarity and fused by a core of "common intelligence."

The idea of "social fusion" is pivotal in James's prefaces to his international fiction, and serves as a key to his own relation to America and Europe. It explains the intention he speaks of in the same letter of 1903 while planning his climactic visit to America: to find the stage of his fiction in "human Anglo-Saxonism, with the American extension." For between America and England communication, in more than one sense of the word, was less limited than elsewhere, and the educated of the two nations, above all, had such a stretch of tradition in common—historical, religious, moral, literary, even after all social and political—that from the very start differences between them were less rigorous than between the educated men of other nations. Yet, his idea of "social fusion" sprang originally from his native American consciousness, not from his Anglo-Saxon consciousness. This is made clear by one of his early letters to Thomas Sergeant Perry, written long before he settled in England, even before his first adult experience of Europe. To be an American, he wrote in 1867, "is an excellent preparation for culture" since, more than other people, Americans are free to "pick and choose" and "claim" their cultural "property" wherever they find it. As one hears him speak of young Americans as "men of the future" and of American writers as leaders toward a "vast intellectual fusion" of the "various National tendencies of the world," one is struck both by the Whitmanesque flavor of his vision and by the uncanny prediction of what was to be a driving force behind his own career. The latter is brought home by the conclusion of the passage: "We must of course have something of our own—something distinctive & homogeneous," the young James wrote, "& I take it that we shall find it in our moral consciousness, our unprecedented spiritual lightness and vigour. In this sense at least we shall have a national *cachet*."[18]

As far as the young James was right in seeing the fusion of "various National tendencies" as part of the American destiny, so far his own cosmopolitanism remained American. "His anglicisms," William James wrote in 1889, "are but 'protective resemblances,'— he's really, I won't say a Yankee, but a native of the James family, and has no other country."[19] Few men knew Henry as intimately as William did, and none surely knew more of the James country.

Clearly, the novelist's detachment from America did not mean conversion to a European or an English point of view. Rather, it was related to what T. S. Eliot has called his "baffling escape from Ideas." It was a matter of both integrity and "lucidity," the quality of mind so central in his thinking as to determine more and more the very structure of his fiction. That, in fact, is the lesson which all his writings teach: his point of view had ceased to be American only so far as it had ceased to be national, local, provincial at all.

Beyond this, James's relation to the two worlds at once separated and linked by the Atlantic can be understood only if the deep moral bias of his international fiction is understood. But it should not be hard to see why William only just hesitated to call him a New Englander. Henry James's ethics are highly individual, highly self-reliant. His very silence on such matters as duty and revealed law, his emphasis on integrity, that most personal of virtues, and on the pragmatic value of lucidity stamp him as an American. Forming the very basis of his moral thinking, the two virtues are so closely allied that one seems to be both the condition and the reward of the other. And what, for instance, could be more Emersonian, in essence if not in phrasing, than the conception of a man's dignity expressed by the hero of the late story of "The Velvet Glove":

You were intellectually...rather abject...if your curiosity (in the grand sense of the term) wasn't worth more to you than your dignity. What *was* your dignity, "anyway," but just the consistency of your curiosity, and what moments were ever so ignoble for you as, under the blighting breath of the false gods, stupid conventions, traditions, examples, your lapses from that consistency?

If James's cosmopolitanism violated the letter of this or that man's Americanism, it did not violate its spirit. Consistent dedication to curiosity and to comparison rewarded him with an awareness of what gods, on both sides of the Atlantic, were false. It gave him a freedom from ephemeral conventions which, far from cutting him off from his origins, allowed him to be an American writer in the most meaningful sense of the term.

 *The Final Vision*

HOWELLS FELT that literary "absenteeism" was an expression of "the modern sense which enlarges one's country to the bounds of civilization," and that James planted "the seeds of an imaginative literature" which, though "taking the four winds of heaven in its boughs," was nevertheless as truly "native to our soil" as any yet known.[1] Such recognition of the deep-seated American bias of the expatriate James might seem to obviate the question why the American James decided to live abroad: he had his reasons, let the matter rest there. But although the reasons of the private citizen are not our business, the reasons of the writer are. For the question of his expatriation bears directly on his work and on the total vision, not only of the international situation, but of life, which it contains.

In the first place, expatriation was in a very real sense a fate imposed on James from without. He himself repeatedly spoke of it in such terms. "Being a cosmopolite is an accident, but one must make the best of it"—thus, in a clairvoyant essay of 1878, he summed up the result of his upbringing at the hands of his peripatetic father.[2] And recurring in his essays on Turgenieff, another

expatriate, the note recalls the deterministic element in his fiction—
in *The Portrait of a Lady, The Wings of the Dove,* and particularly
in *The Ambassadors,* that novel which dramatizes the very growth
of a cosmopolitan sensibility. It recalls Strether's sense that one has
to live as one can though, to be sure, as best, as rightly as, one can.
James also wished to live as rightly as he could, and since in him the
cosmopolitan was the writer, his decision to live abroad was determined by the needs of his work. The "painter of life and manners,"
thus he put it later in the Prefaces, depended inevitably on contrast,
and his particular sense of contrast had been "predetermined" for
him by the "facts" of his early life.[3]

A passage in the *Notebooks,* in which, in 1881, back in New
England for the first time since 1875, he reviewed those six decisive
years, seems to arrest almost the very moment when he recognized
and accepted his fate: "I am 37 years old, I have made my choice,
and God knows that I have now no time to waste," he wrote.

My choice is the old world—my choice, my need, my life. There is no
need for me today to argue about this; it is an inestimable blessing to
me, and a rare good fortune, that the problem was settled long ago,
and that I have now nothing to do but to act on the settlement.... My
work lies there—and with this vast new world, *je n'ai que faire.* One
can't do both—one must choose. No European writer is called upon to
assume that terrible burden, and it seems hard that I should be....
but, Heaven forgive me! I feel as if my time were terribly wasted here![4]

The course which followed was to impose the burden of loneliness
upon him. But loneliness, as he knew, was in any case the writer's
fate.[5] And if the man had to pay for the lucid detachment of the
author, we may sympathize but cannot wish it had been different.
For while it is idle to wonder what he would have done if he had
stayed at home, it is certain that he made the best of the uncomfortable accident of his dislocation.

What he made of it is recorded in his work. But his climactic
return to the United States in 1904, after twenty uninterrupted
years abroad, led him to re-examine the contrast between America

and Europe. It led to certain revisions in his favorite image of the American spirit, the American girl. It led above all to certain formulations which give a sharper edge to his concept of manners and their significance for civilization. What he wrote out of that experience, therefore, may in turn suggest what values so attracted him to the Old World that it became his choice and need for art and life together.

William, afraid that Henry might be shocked by modern America, almost tried to dissuade him from coming, but without success. America, Henry answered, had become "almost as romantic" for him as Europe used to be, and warnings about the possible shocks in store for him were "utterly beside the mark—it being absolutely *for* all that class of phenomena" that he nursed his plans. He wanted "to see everything," see the Middle and the Far West, California and the South, for he hoped to find a new mine of material in "human Anglo-Saxonism, with the American extension." Most of these expectations were fulfilled. James spent almost a year in the United States, traveling as far as Florida and California, fascinated by the various "miracles of American expertness"—from "transcendent" dentistry, from trains equipped with barbershops and typists, to "the *universal* joy of this country," the "so excellent room" complete with "perfect" plumbing, which one could count on "always, everywhere."[6] And the letters, not to speak of the more finished record of his impressions in *The American Scene,* show how deeply absorbed he was by the double sense of being on old familiar ground and at the same time finding everything changed.

And yet, if America was exciting, it was not *for* him. About half a year after his return to England he summed up what remained with him: "I found my native land, after so many years, interesting, formidable, fearsome and fatiguing, and much more difficult to see and deal with" than "I had supposed." It is "an extraordinary world, an altogether huge 'proposition,' as they say there," giving one "an immense impression of material and political power; but almost cruelly charmless" and "calculated to make one crouch, ever afterwards, as cravenly as possible, at Lamb House, Rye —if one happens to have a poor little L.H., R., to crouch in." William's alarm of 1903—"I should hate to have you come and, as a result, feel that you had now *done* with American forever"—had been half justified.[7] But only half. In most of the fiction which James wrote after this climactic visit his focus is unmistakably on America. And if the civilization he portrays is seen from without, if the stories are the products of a cosmopolitanized mind habitually aware of an otherness, America nevertheless remains at the center of his subject.

The theme of the American's return now replaces his earlier theme of the American pilgrim to Europe. One of these stories reads in fact like a symbolical rendering of James's own return and the revelation it brought him. For the reactions of Spencer Brydon in "The Jolly Corner" (1908) can be documented almost point by point with James's letters. In the case of the disfigurement of Brydon's American alter ego by the pursuit of "a million a year" this may not be surprising, but the "muffled vibrations" with which the Europeanized Brydon responds to the appeal of "business," too, have their origin in James's own experience. He too could "vibrate" momentarily. For his lecture on "The Lesson of Balzac," he wrote excitedly to Edmund Gosse, "Indianapolis offers £100 for 50 minutes!" and to somebody else a few days later, "a pound a minute —like Patti!" In America even he could make money, and if he preferred nevertheless to "live a beggar at Lamb House," at least he wanted his biographer to "recall the solid sacrifice" involved.[8]

This may be written with tongue in cheek, but no reader of *The Ambassadors* can doubt that James knew well enough how much the "helpless jelly" of his consciousness had been molded by Europe. In this sense, "The Jolly Corner" can quite properly be spoken of as autobiographical and the final note of pity for Brydon's disfigured alter ego as an expression of James's own sense that the ravaged businessman is no less victim of his conditions and therefore no less worthy of sympathy than an Isabel Archer or a

Strether. Nevertheless, the man Brydon would have been had he stayed in America is "grim," "worn," "ruined" despite his "million a year"; he appeals to the lady's sympathy; the man he has become by living in Europe charms her. Her choice is as clear as James's own choice of Lamb House. If the contrast of values remains undefined, it is because the values themselves are neither clearly moral nor clearly intellectual or aesthetic, though all of these somehow hover in the story as possibilities. "The Jolly Corner" is another example of James's refusal to oppose one cultural value to another, and the most that can be said is that, if the European Brydon has it over the American, it is because the civilization which formed him has more charm—morally, intellectually, aesthetically in one —than that which might have formed him in America.

Spencer Brydon's confrontation with the maimed ghost of the American fate he has escaped, then, is symbolical of James's new vision of American wealth—of the dreary ugliness which, in the letters, he associates with the "vast mechanical, industrial, social, financial" power everywhere in evidence.[9] For although in James's world greed and want had always been important sources of moral corruption, American wealth had enjoyed a striking immunity. Except for a few hints—like the allusions to the vulgarity of Adam Verver's early years of money-making in *The Golden Bowl* or to the unmentionable product on which the wealth of the Newsomes in *The Ambassadors* is founded—its sources had remained unquestioned. Now this has changed, and the chase of the dollar has become a source of corruption just as sophisticated English greed is in *The Wings of the Dove.* Indeed, to the symbol of "The Jolly Corner" another story adds the explicit statement. "A Round of Visits" (1910) ends with a meeting between Mark Monteith, another returning American, and Newton Winch, a former fellow-student whom Monteith remembers as "constitutionally common" but whom he now finds mysteriously changed—refined, intelligent, sensitive. The climactic explanation is that Winch, too, like Brydon's specter, has become the guilty victim of "the ugliness, the bitterness,"

the "sinister strangeness" of the money passion. And the shock of
Monteith's realization looks like an image for James's own shock at
realizing what the wealth of a Milly Theale or a Christopher
Newman implied: "He inexpressively understood, and nothing in
life had ever been so strange and dreadful to him as his thus
helping himself" to "the monstrous sense of his friend's 'education.'
It had been, in its immeasurable action, the education of business, of
which the fruits were all around them."

Between the greeds of London and New York there is, however,
a significant difference, which the genesis of "A Round of Visits"
points up. Why, one might ask, should the money passion which
disfigures Brydon's specter refine Newton Winch? The answer is that
the improvement of Newton Winch, a kind of Fortunate Fall motif
which James recorded in the *Notebooks* in 1899, had originally no
connection with his reappraisal of America. Nor indeed is it the
major theme of "A Round of Visits." That grew out of "the notion
of a young man" (Monteith) who has "some secret sorrow" to tell
and "can't find the *recipient,*" which James first recorded in 1894
and which in 1899 he still thought of incorporating in a story of
London, "the great heartless preoccupied city and society" of *The
Wings of the Dove.* There the idea rested until he found it suitable
for dramatizing his new sense of the tenor of American life. But in
being shifted from London to New York, the scene was given a tone
not hinted at in the earlier notes. The high manners of an old and
well-oiled society were replaced by the callow lack of manners or, in
the words of *The American Scene,* the "complete abolition of *forms,*"
which accompanies the economic and social struggle in America.
This became the central subject of the story: the fact that in his
"round of visits" in gaudy, feverish, impersonal New York Monteith
finds nobody willing to listen to his grief—except finally the Newton
Winch whom guilt has made sensitive to his need.[10] None of the
others has time for sympathy. And since manners are fundamentally a matter of social awareness, they have, therefore, "in a
finer sense, no manners." Manners—thus in "A Round of Visits"—

"didn't matter there—nobody's did." Hence—in "The Jolly Corner"
—"How could any one—of any wit—insist on any one else's
'wanting' to live in New York?"

The idea of manners had indeed much to do with James's
decision to live and work in Europe. More and more, manners had
come to represent for him a crystallization of social experience in
which moral and aesthetic values met—a view implicit already in
Strether's response to Madame de Vionnet's Paris. But James's trip
to America in 1904 brought a new intensity to his concern with the
meaning of manners for civilization. Almost everything he wrote
out of that experience, therefore, adumbrates his sense of their moral
significance. Even the address on "The Question of Our Speech,"
which he delivered before the graduating class at Bryn Mawr in
1905, turned into an essay on manners, a plea for recognition of
their importance as "one of the most precious conquests of civilization, the very core of our social heritage." For speech is part of this
heritage—like matrimony, for example. Therefore: "Abate one jot
of the quantity, and, much more, of the quality, of the consecration
required, and we practically find ourselves emulating the beasts,
who prosper as well without a vocabulary as without a marriage
service."[11]

James no doubt had his eyes on his audience. For his old
favorite, "the delicate, nervous, emancipated young woman begotten
of our institutions" and "equipped with a lovely face and an irritable
moral conscience,"[12] upon close examination had turned out to be
in desperate need of guidance. In story after story she had shamed
the hereditary aristocrats of Europe by her natural nobility; in story
after story he had endowed her with a "moral spontaneity" innocent
of acquired forms which found its foils and enemies among sophisti-
cates whose very *savoir faire* gave warning of a moral void. Now,
after seeing her at home, in the trains going south and west, in
Boston and at Bryn Mawr, his trust in her unaided wisdom is shaken.
Now he recognizes that he has been guilty of idealizing her: creature
of his "incurable prejudice in favour of grace," the "supposedly

typical little figure," he now has to confess, "was of course pure poetry, and had never been anything else." Now, therefore, she comes in for treatment of a consistently different kind. One of the essays of this time, a not so fugitive article on "The Manners of American Women" which ran in four consecutive numbers of *Harper's Bazar* in 1907, reads at times indeed almost like a dressing down intended for Isabel Archer. For, says James now, "the wisdom of the ages has everywhere quite absolved" the woman from "the formidable care of extracting a conception of the universe and a scheme of manners from her moral consciousness alone"— the burden which in America "she has so rashly assumed." This essay, too, is an exposition of the nature of manners, a plea for their high value. And it closes therefore on an appeal to "our sisters" to escape the "fatal trap" of their freedom and their "vast complacencies," to avail themselves of "acquired" knowledge, of the "consecration of discipline"—in a word, of the "economy" of manners.

The "heiress of all the ages" has come a long way. Her princeliness has turned out to be merely the "preposterous" result of her "uncorrected, unrelated state." For in abandoning her to her "crude presumption," to her native "ignorance and folly," the "whole social order" has betrayed her. What indeed can she know, "helpless chit" that she is, "about manners or tone, about proportion or perspective, about modesty or mystery?" Thus James lets her plaintively ask in *The American Scene.*[13] Similarly, in one of the late stories, Julia Bride cries out in protest against the freedom of her juvenile flirtations: "That mother should have insanely *let* me, should so vulgarly have taken it for my natural, my social career—*that's* the disgusting humiliating thing." In "Julia Bride" (1909) James dramatized the education of the American girl to the beauty of dignified social ritual. Engaged to an old-fashioned New Yorker, Julia is embarrassed by her past—"her own six engagements and her mother's three nullified marriages—nine nice distinct little horrors in all." She has learned that while it is one thing "to stare at a girl" till she is bored and to send her the latest novels by the dozen, it is "something quite other to hold open for her, with eyes attached to eyes, the gate, moving on such stiff silver hinges, of the grand square forecourt of the palace of wedlock." Rhythm and imagery of the passage suggest the courtliness of a ritual dance. And indeed Julia blushes when she thinks how "her younger romps" have dishonored the stately "forecourt" of betrothal, how she has "tumbled over the wall with this, that and the other raw playmate," playing " 'tag' and leap-frog" verily "from corner to corner." For she has come to see that "the high ceremony and dignity and decency, above all the grand gallantry and finality" of her fiancé represent a real delicacy of feeling.

Despite its comic tone, James's treatment of the American girl goes to the very center of his view of manners. As early as 1892 he had noted "the growing divorce between the American woman (with her comparative leisure, culture, grace, social instincts, artistic ambitions) and the male American immersed in the ferocity of business." It had then seemed to him that this divorce was in a fair way to become "an abyss of inequality." Now, after observing the whole extent of the damage, he has come to see the "unrelated state" of the American girl as her "uncorrected" state, the source of her crudity of manners. Interestingly, this is exactly the view he took of the "unfriended" state of American speech. As he explained in his Bryn Mawr address,

whereas the great idioms of Europe in general have grown up at home and in the family, the ancestral circle (with their migrations all comfortably prehistoric), our transported maiden, our unrescued Andromeda ... was to be disjoined from all the associations, the other presences, that had attended her, that had watched for her and with her, that had helped to form her manners and her voice, her taste and her genius.

And manners, conceived finely enough, turned into virtue: "the art of meeting life finely," he said in *Harper's Bazar,* is "the art of preparations"; therefore, "it is well to have had as many things as possible discriminated and thought out and tried and tested for us."[14] Virtue, indeed, was ultimately a distillation of experience and reflection, but a distillation of *social* experience—a "social grace and value."

The last phrase comes from a passage in *A Small Boy and Others* which shows the origin of this empirical concept of morality: "As I reconsider both my own and my brother's early start," James wrote in his late sixties,

> it is quite for me as if the authors of our being and guardians of our youth had virtually said to us but one thing, directed our course but by one word, though constantly repeated: Convert, convert, convert! ... We were to convert and convert, success—in the sense that was in the general air—or no success; and simply everything that should happen to us, every contact, every impression and every experience we should know, were to form our soluble stuff; with only ourselves to thank should we remain unaware, by the time our perceptions were decently developed, of the substance finally projected and most desirable. That substance might be just consummately Virtue, as a social grace and value—and as a matter furthermore on which pretexts for ambiguity of view and measure were as little as possible called upon to flourish.... the moral of all of which was [thus James concludes the paragraph] that we need never fear not to be good enough if we were only social enough: a splendid meaning indeed being attached to the latter term.[15]

Though it is neither necessary nor reasonable and safe to read James's fiction as allegory on his father's mystical theories of the "social redemption of man,"[16] it is difficult to exaggerate the importance of this passage for both the origin and the nature of his thinking. Manners ultimately represented for him quite simply a moral knowledge derived empirically, a "substance finally projected" by the social experience of the race. And the method of his late fiction, particularly of the three great novels of his maturity, constitutes a symbolical rendering of the process. For like the manners "finally projected" by history, the moral consciousness "finally projected" by his fiction constituted in his vision of life "Virtue, as a social grace and value."

But if the place of manners in James's view of art and life owes much to his early upbringing, it also goes far toward explaining why he "preferred" Europe. For one thing, he simply liked what William James once called "the *attained* social character of European civilizations"; it was more stimulating to the particular discriminations he was after—since they were what he was most capable of— than the as yet more "thinly-composed" society of his own country. Moreover, though the "great modern collapse of all the forms" and "restraints and mysteries" might, as he noted in 1895, be on its way in Europe too, it was slower there than in the America of the Gilded Age, and he preferred the old tranquillities to the callow modern rush. This is made clear by some of his late stories, by "Julia Bride" and "Crapy Cornelia," for instance, which rest on the contrast between the "formidable," "bristling" America he found in 1904 and the more decorous and gentler one which he had known thirty years before and which, so Edith Wharton said, still lingered, paradoxically, in Europe. Above all, however, the Europe of American travelers, pilgrims, colonists, in a word, the Europe of the "international situation," was the scene of a conflict of manners essential to his enterprise. This is doubtless the meaning behind a confession he made in 1913—that in Europe "a certain part of the work of discrimination and selection and primary clearing of the ground" was already done for him so that he could begin "further on" than in America, where much of his time would have been consumed by preliminary "sifting and selecting."[17] What he was speaking of was the work of the novelist whose love of contrast had ended in a pragmatic search for the constituents of civilization.

It was the work he had pursued from early years to late. In Bonn in 1860, the boy of seventeen had noted that German high-school students, if on an average "not so acute or clever as their brothers" in America, were much more "comely mannered."[18] Time was to deepen and to clarify this observation. American acuteness, cleverness, "character," was to emerge as the presumptuous intelligence of an Isabel Archer, as the destructive crudity of a George Flack, and later still as the tragic spiritual beauty of a Milly Theale; the comely manners of the boys in Bonn were to grow variously into the rich beauty of a Marie de Vionnet or the steely polish of a Kate Croy. One was to learn that innocence and experience both were capable of good and evil. And one was to imagine the social face of a civilization alive with spiritual strength, yet chastened and made stronger by social discipline. If the return to America forced certain revisions in the portrait of the American girl, the reason was that the Isabel Archers and Milly Theales were the creatures of an earlier time. Yet the memories of that time were too vivid to be entirely erased by later observations. Even the story of Julia Bride, therefore, closes on "the high note" of her "wonderful composition," which prevents her, Isabel Archer-like, from shutting her eyes to the "grim lucidity" of her new self-knowledge.

Indeed, to the very end James imaged the contrast between America and Europe as a contrast between the complementary values of spiritual spontaneity and social experience. His vision was clearly American, and it is ultimately idle to question its objective truth beyond the obvious. For while he began as the chronicler of an international situation which was part of history, and of American history in particular, in time the realist turned symbolist, almost romancer in Hawthorne's sense of the term. The historian of an international situation which had never been anything but an American situation turned into the historian of the human situation, of civilization pure and simple. True, the American character remained his lifelong preoccupation; but the "situation" he served as recorder, the character he served as interpreter, both in turn had to serve his deeper purpose. For—to adapt his own words about Flaubert—listening "at the chamber of the soul," in the end he "floated on a deeper tide" than the tide of current and local history.[19]

This is made clear by the three great symbolical novels of his maturity. It is made clear too by the history of his last, unfinished novel, which might have equaled them.[20] *The Ivory Tower* (1917) treats once more of an American's return and of his confrontation with the corruptive money passion. But the symbolic specter of "The Jolly Corner" is now replaced by vivid living figures recalling Densher and Kate Croy of *The Wings of the Dove*—by Horton Vint, one of the unfaithful stewards recurring in James's late fiction, and Cissy Foy, a "poor" and clever girl with a great "sense of life," living "in a society of the rich" and "more or less by their bounty." It may appear surprising that while aware of the risk of repeating the figure of Charlotte Stant, James should not have thought of Densher and Kate, who seem closer to Vint and Cissy. But *The Ivory Tower* resembles *The Golden Bowl* in a more important respect: though with a new emphasis derived from James's reappraisal of America, it was to dramatize once more the fusion of "character" and "culture," of American idealism and European form.

What brings Graham Fielder, the hero of the novel, back to America is the desire of his uncle, Mr. Betterman, to atone for a life of "ferocious acquisition." In a revulsion reminiscent of those earlier revulsions of Christopher Newman and Adam Verver, Mr. Betterman wishes to devote his millions to the support of a force totally different from the one which has created them. But he is wiser than Verver: realizing that having *been* business all his life, he himself "can't be anything else," he makes over the fruits of acquisition to a man who knows nothing of how they have been acquired. He leaves his fortune to Fielder just because the young man knows nothing of "the mystery of the 'market'" and has never done even "three cents' worth of business." And when Fielder confesses that there is in fact nothing whatever he can *do,* this is precisely what Mr. Betterman's purpose demands: "the question," he tells him, "isn't of your doing, but simply of your being." For after a life spent all in doing, Mr. Betterman has arrived at what Henry James, Sr., had taught his sons—that being a good man was career enough. Therefore, by simply being that, by "finding it impossible to do what *they* do," all those absorbed in making money, Fielder will do

enough *for* them. But though Betterman is wiser than Verver, he is
not wise enough. The fruits of evil can have no part in the atonement. And the rejection of the tycoon's atonement—in *The Golden
Bowl* suggested only by the irony in the treatment of Adam Verver
—now becomes James's central thematic concern. As far as James's
notes allow one to guess, after Mr. Betterman's death, Fielder was
to make over the administration of his fortune to Horton Vint, who
was to cheat him of it. And Fielder, realizing the betrayal, was to
do nothing about it since, considering "the history of the money,"
this would be "the most congruous way" of "resigning it to its
natural associations."

This indictment of the "awful game of grab" is typical of
James's representation of America after 1904, but it is not the whole
representation. The Europeanized Fielder is balanced by Rosanna
Gaw, the last of James's American girls; and the novel was to close,
apparently, on a union of the two, representing a wisdom uniting
culture and idealism, the virtues of Europe and America. Rosanna,
however, shows the impact of James's late vision of his native
country. To make her capable of carrying the full weight of his
symbolic intention, James could not expose her to comparison with
a Daisy Miller or a Julia Bride. Hence she is pointedly unmodern:
"she loathes self-exhibition; she loathes being noticed; she loathes
every form of publicity." She is even without the grace and beauty
which Milly Theale and Maggie Verver share with their less princely
sisters; she is "large loose ponderous," a "plain quiet daughter,"
specifically clumsy in her motions. Above all, however, wealthy as
she is, Rosanna "loathes every separate dollar she possesses." She
has lost Milly's and Maggie's unquestioning acceptance of wealth,
for her knowledge of its "natural associations" is complete. In sum,
she is a new figure in James's gallery of Americans, distinguished
from the world surrounding her as well as from his earlier symbols
of American innocence. Yet from the Europeanized Fielder, too, she
is set off: her "amplitude" somehow never finds "the right measure";
she is "massive" but "essentially unobservant of forms." In this, if in

nothing else, she is still the sister of those late figures whose function in James's international world it was to symbolize the lack of social discipline.

At James's death, *The Ivory Tower* was left unfinished, the outlines of the union of Rosanna Gaw and Gray Fielder were left vague. Under the pressure of the Great War James felt that he could not go on with the subject, and his life came to an end before the war did. But his agonized reaction to the tragic "plunge of civilization into this abyss of blood and darkness"[21] in 1914 constituted no rejection of the vision which had grown in him so steadily. His deepest concern had finally been with the possibilities of man, not with his actualities. No war was needed to make the author of *The Wings of the Dove* aware how thin the crust of civilization is, how deep the bondage of men to dark and ugly things. And if in 1914 James had to lay aside *The Ivory Tower* because the wrath of the time was too violent for imagining the symbolic union of Rosanna Gaw and Gray Fielder, the very passion of his agony shows how incurable was his belief, not in the achieved reality, but in man's need, of a civilization fusing idealism and discipline, spirit and form.

N otes

PROLOGUE

1. *The Letters of Henry James,* ed. Percy Lubbock (New York, 1920), I, 13.

2. Quoted in Howard Mumford Jones, *America and French Culture 1750-1848* (Chapel Hill, 1927), p. 296. "In 1820 only 30 per cent of American publications were by native authors; in 1840, 50 per cent, though school books, extensively produced in the thirties, account in part for the increase" (*ibid.*). The early Harvard curriculum was "a block of European thought transplanted bodily to America" (*ibid.,* p. 20). For the influence of the colleges and universities after the middle of the nineteenth century, see Howard Mumford Jones, *The Theory of American Literature* (Ithaca, 1948), ch. iv. Emerson's concise statement is contained in the opening sentence of his lecture on "The Young American."

3. Quoted in Constance Rourke, *American Humor: A Study of the National Character* (Garden City, 1953), p. 142. [1st ed. 1931].

4. Oliver Wendell Holmes, *Our Hundred Days in Europe* (Boston and New York, 1888), pp. 310-13, *passim.*

5. R. W. Emerson, *English Traits* (Boston and New York, 1884), p. 225. Mark Twain is quoted in A. B. Paine, *Mark Twain, A Biography* (New York, 1912), II, 470; see also A .B. Paine, ed., *Mark Twain's Letters, Arranged with Comment* (New York, 1917), I, 201.

6. George Francis Train, *An American Merchant in Europe, Asia, and*

Australia: A Series of Letters... (New York, 1857), pp. vii-viii, 342-54, *passim.* That Train was devoid of any sense of intellectual tradition is evident throughout but made rather startlingly clear in this passage: "... what are Americans but Englishmen left to themselves. Islanders, Asiatics, Africans and Europeans, have no community of feeling with, and [are] all widely different from the children of the Anglo-Saxon father" (pp. 342-43). It may be worth noting that Train's passages dealing with the Holy Land bear a certain similarity to *Innocents Abroad.* The following is typical: "I have been to Jerusalem, and have returned again, delighted and disgusted; delighted while traveling in the hallowed associations of by-gone ages—disgusted at the utter desolation of nature. My ride was tedious, my lunch bad, my horse sore-footed and sore-backed" (p. 292). This is displeasure over inconvenience set down without humorous or critical intent. The similarity to Mark Twain is in substance only, not in manner or attitude.

7. Holmes, *op. cit.,* p. 200. James, *Hawthorne* (London, 1879), p. 45.

8. "The French and Italian Notebooks by Nathaniel Hawthorne," ed. Norman Holmes Pearson (Doctoral dissertation, Yale, 1941), III, 579-80, *passim;* quoted with the editor's permission. (This is the only complete edition.) *Letters of Charles Eliot Norton* (Boston and New York, 1913), I, 398.

9. Stanley T. Williams, "Cosmopolitanism in American Literature Before 1880," in Margaret Denny and William H. Gilman, eds., *The American Writer and the European Tradition* (Minneapolis, 1950), p. 61; R. P. Blackmur, "The American Literary Expatriate," in David F. Bowers, ed., *Foreign Influences in American Life* (Princeton, 1944), pp. 134-35.

10. Henry James, *William Wetmore Story and His Friends* (Edinburgh and London, 1903), I, 5-6, 312-13.

11. Preface to Vol. XVIII of the New York Edition; see *The Art of the Novel,* ed. R. P. Blackmur (New York, 1934), p. 280.

12. *French Poets and Novelists* (London, 1893), p. 243 [1st ed. 1878].

CHAPTER I

1. Carl Becker, *The Declaration of Independence: A Study in The History of Political Ideas* (New York, 1940), p. 128.

2. William Hazlitt, *Complete Works,* ed. P. P. Howe (London and Torronto, 1932), XI, 183.

3. See the prefaces to *The American* and *The Ambassadors,* in *The Art of the Novel,* ed. R. P. Blackmur (New York, 1934), pp. 24, 316. For reasons of convenience all references to James's prefaces to the New York Edition will be to this collection.

4. *Bracebridge Hall,* rev. ed. (New York, 1849), p. 365.

5. *Wolfert's Roost and Other Papers* (New York, 1868), p. 357.

6. *The Crayon Miscellany,* rev. ed. (New York, 1849), pp. 216-17.

7. *North American Review,* XV (1822), 214. A contemporary review of *The Alhambra* makes this particularly clear by linking Irving's English and Spanish sketches with the earlier Knickerbocker writings of his own New York: "We have been with him" along the Hudson, by England's "ancient piles," and now to the "old cities and romantic towers" of Spain. "We are *there* actually, while reading the Alhambra" (New York *Mirror,* June 23, 1832, quoted in Stanley Williams, *The Life of Washington Irving* [New York, 1935], II, 317).

8. For instance in Train's *An American Merchant in Europe, Asia, and Australia* (1851); see Prologue, n. 6 above. But the same is true of W. C. Bryant's *The Picturesque Souvenir: Letters of a Traveller; or, Notes of Things Seen in Europe and America* (1851).

9. Paulding, even after opening his *Sketch of Old England, by a New England Man* (1822) with the announcement that he would avoid old castles, cathedrals, and other monuments described already "upwards of six thousand times," described just such castles, sometimes indeed "book in hand," because of the interest which they derived even for him from their association with "little historical romances"; see especially I, 2, 100, 101. For another example see n. 16 below.

10. See J. T. Hatfield, *New Light On Longfellow* (Boston and New York, 1933), p. 28.

11. *Outre-Mer: A Pilgrimage Beyond the Sea* (Boston and New York, 1886), p. 30.

12. *Outre-Mer,* pp. 233-34. The letter to his mother is quoted in Lawrance Thompson, *Young Longfellow* (New York, 1938), p. 118. Mark Twain's passage on the "historical creek" begins: "It is popular to admire the Arno." (*Innocents Abroad* [New York: Harper & Brothers, n.d.] I, 253).

13. The phrase comes from *Hyperion* (Boston and New York, 1886), p. 175. Large portions of *Outre-Mer* deal with literary subjects Longfellow was at the time teaching at Bowdoin. When a second stay in Europe, made in preparation for taking over Ticknor's chair of modern languages at Harvard, led to *Hyperion* (1839), he almost doubled the proportion of similar material. Although in fictional form it deals with much more personal matters, *Hyperion* was to do for Germany what *Outre-Mer* had done for the Latin countries. But much as Longfellow maintained that in order to "feel the popular poetry" of the country one had to be familiar with its landscape (p. 114), German life and scenery are so much subordinated to the "glorious world of poetry, romance, and dreams" that in *Hyperion,* too, little is left of actual observation. For Longfellow again tailored his report to a fashion and dressed it up with learning.

14. *Mark Twain's Letters,* ed. A. B. Paine (New York and London, 1917), I, 208; *Innocents Abroad* (New York and London, n.d.), I, 98; A. B. Paine, *Mark Twain, A Biography* (New York, 1912), I, 466. An excellent statement of Mark Twain's attitude toward Europe in *Innocents Abroad* is to be found in John C. McCloskey, "Mark Twain as Critic in *The Innocents Abroad,*" *American Literature,* XXV (1953), 139-51.

15. *Authorship, A Tale* (Boston, 1830), pp. 3-5. The first few pages of this semiautobiographical tale constitute an essay on Westminster Abbey which may have been published separately before being incorporated in *Authorship*. In the introduction to his edition of *American Writers: A Series of Papers Contributed to Blackwood's Magazine (1824-1825) by John Neal* (Durham, N. C., 1937), F. L. Pattee assigns an excerpt from it to the *United States Literary Gazette* of April 1, 1824. This is erroneous; the *United States Literary Gazette* of 1824 does not contain the passage.

16. See H. M. Jones, *America and French Culture 1750-1848* (Chapel Hill, 1927), p. 280. R. E. Spiller's *The American in England* (New York, 1926) gives an idea of the number of such records published during "the first half century of independence." Horace Greeley's *Glances at Europe* (1851) may serve as example. Describing his book as "a clear and vivid daguerreotype of the districts I traversed" (p. iv), Greeley deals with topography, agriculture, technology, and, from a democratic humanitarian point of view, with the admittedly "more obvious social characteristics" (p. iv). He, too, is unimpressed with the notorious Abbey; occasionally he boldly tries for humor ("They have something they call sun over here which they show occasionally, but which looks more like a boiled turnip than it does like its American namesake"—p. 46). But for humor New York was not up to Nevada, and Greeley is on the whole so tritely conscientious that he can hardly be considered one of Mark Twain's forerunners; though consciously unromantic, he is no satirist. But that his news-letters and other such series (e. g., Bryant's) could first run in the leading dailies and then sell collected in book form is proof of the American appetite for impressions of the "Old World."

17. But American self-esteem could take the form of pride in the magnificence of nature, as in Mark Twain's boastful comparison of Lake Tahoe with Lake Como (in *Innocents Abroad*) or Melville's preference for the Hudson over the Rhine (in his *Journal of a Visit to London and the Continent, 1849-1850,* ed. E. M. Metcalf [Cambridge, 1948], p. 66). Into such comparisons, too, the appreciation of Europe's historical monuments could enter, however, as when Parkman, the historian, in his novel *Vassall Morton* (1856), said that the ruined castles of the Rhine "with the memories about them, turn the tables dead against" the Hudson so that Americans had better "make the best" of their "feeling for nature" (pp. 112-13). In "The Impressions of a Cousin" James made his narrator, an American artist recently returned from Europe, write in her diary: "This place is very lovely, and the Hudson is as beautiful as the Rhine. There are the words, in black and white, over my signature: I can't do more than that. I have said it a dozen times, in answer to as many challenges, and now I record the opinion with all the solemnity I can give it. May it serve for the rest of the summer" (*Century Magazine,* XXVII [December, 1883], 262). This "international" note is not necessary to either plot or theme, but apparently springs from the desire for "actuality" which James mentions in pondering the story in the *Notebooks* (p. 52). Add that he composed the story during his visit

to America in 1883 or immediately afterward, and you suspect that the comparison of Hudson and Rhine was commonplace.

18. The subtitle, *Parts of a Life Else Untold,* may hint at autobiographical significance. A fuller discussion of *Paul Fane* and of this whole aspect of Willis' fiction is to be found in my article on "Social Criticism of Europe in the Fiction of N. P. Willis," *American Literature,* XX (November, 1948), 313-22, on which I have here drawn.

19. See *A Letter to His Countrymen* (New York, 1834), p. 12; *Gleanings in Europe: England,* ed. R. E. Spiller (New York, 1930), pp. 153, 154.

20. *Correspondence of James Fenimore Cooper* (New Haven, 1922), I, 171. Cooper's determination to "carry away accurate notions of physical things" (*The Heidenmauer,* Mohawk Edition [New York and London, 1895], p. 85) often played him false. "From the habit of analyzing buildings," he says for instance in his description of St. Peter's, "I counted the paces as I advanced, and knew how far I was within the pile" (*Gleanings in Europe: Italy* [Philadelphia, 1838], II, 66); but here, as so often in his travel books, the accurate fact fails to convey a vivid impression. And the minute descriptions of the manners of high society, the preoccupation with the minutiae of purely conventional regulations of social behavior with which his two books on France and England are filled, now have little interest save as documents of a period. But that they had contemporary interest is suggested by Holmes's statement in 1886: "I know full well that many readers would be disappointed if I did not mention some of the grand places and bring in some of the great names that lend their lustre to London society" (*Our Hundred Days in Europe,* p. 69).

21. His European novels contain no Johns, or Giacomos, or Hanses; only noblemen, servants, priests—that is, social types. Mark Twain's statement that Cooper "saw nearly all things as through a glass eye, darkly" applies here too.

22. For Adams, Jefferson, Emerson, Thoreau, Eliot, Howells see E. H. Cady, *The Gentleman in America* (Syracuse, 1949), pp. 95, 100-101, 162, 164. For Margaret Fuller see Philip Rahv, ed., *Discovery of Europe* (Boston, 1947), p. 162; for Melville see *Pierre* (New York, 1949), p. 8, and *Moby Dick,* ch. xxvi; for Lowell see *Ode,* Sec. VI. The natural aristocrat could go under different names, but the phrase "Nature's nobleman" seems to have been something of a cliché. In 1851, New York saw the performance of a play under this title, a comedy dealing with the incognito visit of an English earl to America and ending with his marriage to a young American woman. But the point of the whole thing is summarized in the epilogue which she addresses to the audience:

> Not for the sake of wealth or vain display,
> 'Tis love, not pride, that beckons me away;
> I give my heart, and blame me if you can,
> Not to the peer—but NATURE'S NOBLEMAN.

Cooper's theory of natural nobility, however, differs considerably from the theories of the other Americans cited. As Cady has shown, Cooper modified the idea of natural talent by a theory of "gifts" which formed "a new basis for exclusiveness," reconcilable with democracy only in Cooper's own "highly technical sense" of the term, since only "life-long association" with the "class of gentlemen" could produce these "gifts" (p. 125). One suspects that such "rationalizations of 'good birth,'" as Cady calls them (p. 20), are related to the high value which Cooper, unlike Jefferson, for instance, placed on foreign travel. They must account also for the emphasis on family lineage which distinguishes Cooper from Melville. Melville's protest against the notion of the "monarchical world" that "in demagoguical America" all things "irreverently seethe and boil in the vulgar caldron of an everlasting uncrystalizing Present" (*Pierre*, p. 7) might with some justice have been addressed to Cooper, who emphasized just that notion in *Home as Found*. Melville could inveigh against those who, like the Effinghams of *Home as Found*, returned from Europe with a supercilious contempt for their own countrymen; like Jefferson, he could see dangers in "enlarged foreign travel" (*ibid.*, p. 256). Such warnings against an experience which one might think broadening may be difficult to understand. But it is one of the ironies of Cooper's case—of the shift of his emphasis from *political* democracy to *social* views anything but democratic—to suggest how little without reason such warnings were in those years, when this "new country" was exposed to influences hostile to its new government and hostile above all to its experiment in a new social order. It is perhaps an irony inherent in the American predicament of the time.

23. Compare, for instance, James's Bessie Alden in "An International Episode" with Cooper's Grace Van Cortlandt and Tom Howel in *Home as Found*.

24. *Home as Found*, Mohawk Edition (New York, 1896), pp. 223, 226.

25. *Ibid.*, pp. iv, 184. See also p. 54. The notorious James passage occurs in *Hawthorne* (London, 1879), pp. 43-45. It is only fair to add that in *Notions of the Americans* Cooper had spoken of the absence of "manners" as an "obstacle against which American literature has to contend" (II, 108). In 1828 in Europe he still felt that the bane of the American artist was the blessing of the American citizen. Ultimately "the poverty of the materials" with which the American writer has to contend is due to the fact that the "darkest ages" of American history "are illuminated by the light of truth" (II, 109). Cooper's position here is similar to Hawthorne's in the preface to *The Marble Faun*. But after his return to America he came to see the absence of "manners" not only as an obstacle to literature, but as a danger to society. For discussions of Cooper's dilemma and of certain links between Cooper and James, see two articles by Marius Bewley, "Revaluations (XVI): James Fenimore Cooper," *Scrutiny*, XIX (1952-53), 98-125, and "Fenimore Cooper and the Economic Age," *American Literature*, XXVI (1954), 166-95. Both are highly suggestive but underplay the significant differences between Cooper's narrowly social and political concerns and James's moral ones.

26. The idea is central in the address on "The Question of Our Speech"

which James delivered to the graduating class at Bryn Mawr in June, 1905. See *The Question of Our Speech. The Lesson of Balzac: Two Lectures* (Boston, 1905), p. 14.

27. *The Diverting History of John Bull and Brother Jonathan,* by Hector Bull-Us. New Edition (New York, 1835), p. 172. James's remark is to be found in the *Notebooks,* eds. F. O. Matthiessen and K. B. Murdock (New York, 1947), p. 167.

28. Trevelyan's anecdote is quoted by the Earl of Halifax in "Anglo-American Relations," the Fifth Montague Burton Lecture on International Relations, University of Leeds, 1947. For the remark by Bret Harte see the *Overland Monthly,* I (1868), 101; for Smalley see *London Letters and Some Others* (New York, 1891), II, 345; and for Holmes *Our Hundred Days in Europe,* p. 78. In August, 1957, when Red Skelton, the comedian, returned from Europe, the Associated Press reported that Skelton had taken his son to Europe "to give him a chance to 'see some of the wonderful places he had read about.' " See for instance *Register-Guard,* Eugene, Ore., August 5, 1957, p. 2A.

29. An English reviewer of the mid-fifties, for example, finds Longfellow "like most Americans" deeply impressed by the "relics of old days" and *Hyperion,* therefore, a collection of "fancies" rather than a report on German life (*Chamber's Journal,* XXII [1854], 310-13). Another points to Willis' "childish" eagerness in following Childe Harold's tracks and to the naïve partiality of his comments on England (*Edinburgh Review,* LXII [1836], 351-56). Even when a reviewer is in sympathy with the political thesis of an American, as the *Westminster Review* was with Cooper's, he cannot help remarking that the American's cases in point, like Cooper's oppressed Venice in *The Bravo,* are of the past (*Westminster Review,* XVI [1832], 182). Nor do the Continental reviews, as far as I have been able to ascertain, differ in these respects from the English.

30. "They first frame an hypothesis, by which they prove men to be wolves, and then treat them as if they really were such" (Robert Coram, *Political Inquiries* ... [Wilmington, 1791], p. iv). For Barlow see *The Columbiad, a Poem* (Philadelphia, 1809), I, viii, xiii; see also the Argument to Book VIII (II, 74). For Paine see *Writings,* ed. Moncure D. Conway (New York and London, 1894), II, 404. The passage occurs in Paine's Introduction to Part II. These and related formulations of the early Republic are discussed in C. A. and M. R. Beard, *The American Spirit: A Study of the Idea of Civilization in the United States* (New York, 1942), ch. iv.

31. *The Bravo,* Mohawk Edition (New York and London, 1895), p. 413.

32. See Gilbert Chinard, "Eighteenth-Century Theories on America as a Human Habitat," *Proceedings of the American Philosophical Society,* XCI (1947), 27-57.

33. *Letters of Mrs. Adams, The Wife of John Adams* (Boston, 1840), pp. 253, 358.

34. Jefferson's letter is to be found in Rahv, *op. cit.,* p. 54. For Coram see *Political Inquiries,* p. 75.

35. *The Works of John Adams,* ed. Charles Francis Adams (Boston, 1850-56), III, 170-71.

36. Adams, *loc. cit.* James's preliminary "project" for *The Ambassadors,* from which I quote, is printed in *The Notebooks;* see p. 396. J. J. Firebaugh has pointed out James's pragmatic approach to morals in *The Awkward Age;* see "The Pragmatism of Henry James," *Virginia Quarterly Review,* XXVII (1951), 419-35. One of Firebaugh's formulations is particularly applicable in the present context: the statement that James's pragmatism involved "truth for men, not Truth for Man." More recently Marius Bewley has pointed to the pragmatism of *The Golden Bowl* (see *The Complex Fate* [London, 1952], p. 148).

37. *Hawthorne,* p. 162. An extended study of certain links between James and Hawthorne is to be found in four essays which Marius Bewley published in *Scrutiny* in 1949 and 1950 and which, with additions, are collected in his *The Complex Fate* (London, 1952). While this suggestive book is full of the kind of illuminating insight that comes from sensitive reading, in it Bewley has allowed his imagination a maximum of autonomy. He mixes highly perceptive comment with rash generalization—perhaps because he has succumbed to the temptation of the influence study (the original title of three of the essays was "James's Debt to Hawthorne"), his particular thesis being that "Hawthorne was the great American predecessor, the *only* one through whose art [James] approached his own native tradition" (*The Complex Fate,* p. 5; italics mine), and that it is fatuous to insist, "to any considerable extent, on the influences of Flaubert, Turgenev, Maupassant, and Zola" (*ibid.,* p. 10). It is indeed possible to exaggerate the exclusiveness of "influences"; though Hawthorne told James much about America, James learned of the traditions of his native land through many channels besides the work of Hawthorne.

38. See Hawthorne's letter to Ticknor in Caroline Ticknor, *Hawthorne and His Publisher* (Boston, 1913), p. 206; *Doctor Grimshawe's Secret* (Boston, 1883), p. 211; *Our Old Home* (Boston, 1883), p. 83; *Grimshawe,* pp. 180-81. In *Our Old Home* he confesses, too, that while viewing Shakespeare's house he was "conscious of not the slightest emotion" (p. 123). Except where I now have to disagree, I here freely draw on my more detailed discussion of "Europe in Hawthorne's Fiction," *ELH,* XIV (1947), 219-45.

39. *Grimshawe,* p. 253; see also pp. 199-200.

40. "The French and Italian Notebooks," ed. Norman Holmes Pearson (Doctoral dissertation, Yale, 1941), III, 579-80; quoted with the permission of the editor. "A Look Into Hawthorne's Workshop: Being Notes for a Posthumous Romance," *Century Magazine,* XXV (1883), 434.

41. *Hawthorne,* p. 165.

42. *The Marble Faun* (Boston, 1883), p. 207.

43. *Ibid.,* p. 276.

44. See *Our Old Home,* p. 256; James's *Notebooks,* p. 28; *Hawthorne and His Publisher,* p. 214; see also pp. 229, 233, 236, 241; Hawthorne's letters to James T. Fields in Fields's *Yesterdays with Authors* (Boston and New York,

1900), pp. 8-84, *passim;* and the letter from Hawthorne to Longfellow quoted in Holmes, *Our Hundred Days in Europe*, p. 311.

45. *Hawthorne and His Publisher*, p. 241.

46. "Occasional Paris," in *Portraits of Places* (New York, 1948), p. 115. The essay was first published under the title of "Paris Revisited" in January, 1878, in the *Galaxy.*

47. See *Transatlantic Sketches* (Boston, 1875), pp. 7, 13-14. James's first reaction to England was far from simple. And to interpret his later criticism of the English as due to the disillusionment of an idolator who found his gods "nodding on their dilapidated thrones" (Van Wyck Brooks, *The Pilgrimage of Henry James* [New York, 1925], p. 151) is simply to misinterpret the meaning of his whole career. It is healthy amusement to follow Matthiessen's arrangement of William's and Henry's early letters (in *The James Family* [New York, 1947], pp. 286-314), for from the text alone it is sometimes impossible to tell whether the future "exile" or the stout American is speaking. Like other Americans, each of the brothers could be attracted by an environment which, unlike "this naked vacuous America," assails "your every sense and interest," by a Europe "made what it is by men staying in their homes and fighting stubbornly generation after generation for all the beauty, comfort and order that they have got"—thus not Henry but William; each could in turn, again like countless others, be repelled by "this blasted Europe," by its "dinginess and rattiness" and "the extraordinary fixedness and sacredness of the superfluous and the very short measure of the necessary"—thus Henry. If in these particular comments the alignment is not what might be expected, select different letters and it will be reversed. The point is that both—that Henry too—shared in the ambivalence which characterized the American attitude toward England. Nor toward England alone. Henry's first adult letter from Paris, two months after London, included references to the Napoleonic "monotony of glaring would-be monumental spendour" and to "the stagnant gulfs of misery to be seen in two great capitals like London and Paris." Even his ecstatic response to Italy could be interrupted by moments of a deep "loathing" of the "hideous heritage of the past," moments when he felt as if he should like to devote his life "to laying railroads, and erecting blocks of stores on the most classic and romantic sites"—feelings which had their low reverberations in such early stories as "Travelling Companions," in which Americans catch glimpses of the misery behind the "enchanting romance" of Italy.

D8. See *Transatlantic Sketches*, pp. 272-73; *The Letters of Henry James*, ed. Percy Lubbock (New York, 1920), I, 24. F. O. Matthiessen was only partly right when he said that James learned the meaning of *picturesque* from Italian art (*Henry James: The Major Phase*, p. 154). True, the Italian parts of *Transatlantic Sketches* are literally stuffed with descriptions and discussions of paintings and painters. But although the word *picturesque* is constantly on his lips, James very rarely applies it to paintings. There are probably exceptions to this rule that I have overlooked, but the only one I am aware of uses the term specifically to distinguish the German art of Holbein from Italian art (see p. 352). At any rate, while James's long-standing interest in the pictorial was greatly stimulated by Italian art, he usually reserves the term *picturesque* for actual scenes—the kind, for instance, that Piranesi liked to render in his drawings. The sketch from Florence cited above serves as an example, and the same thing is unmistakable in the letter written on his first day in Rome. The point may be piddling, but to see it accurately is to see how much James's first reactions were like the reactions of earlier Americans. It is to see him, for instance, under the spell of something not very different from the aggregation of ruins, ivy, and lichens the lack of which in America Hawthorne had both deplored and praised in the preface to *The Marble Faun.*

49. See *Letters,* I, 57, 391. Hawthorne wrote in *Our Old Home* that in Lincoln he would gladly have felt himself "released from further thraldom to the Cathedral," but "it had taken possession of me," he says almost plaintively, "and would not let me be at rest; so at length I found myself compelled to climb the hill again between daylight and dusk" (p. 182).

50. Cornelia Pulsifer Kelley traces these derivations in *The Early Development of Henry James* (Urbana, 1930).

51. "The Last of the Valerii," *Atlantic Monthly,* XXXIII (January, 1874), 77.

52. *Portraits of Places,* pp. 88-89, 264-65; also p. 279. The contrast between the "Transatlantic Sketches" of the early 1870's and the "Portraits of Places" of the late is made clear by the following two passages: "I think that, in general . . . you are very likely to find a people on your travels what you found them described to be under the mysterious woodcut in some Peter Parley-task-book or play-book of your childhood. The French are a light, pleasure-loving people; ten years of the Boulevards bring no essential amendment to the phrase. The Germans are heavy and fair-haired, deep drinkers and strong thinkers; a fortnight at Homburg doesn't reverse the formula. The only thing to be said is that, as you grow older, French lightness and German weightiness become more complex ideas" ("Homburg Reformed," *Transatlantic Sketches,* p. 361; originally published in the *Nation* of August 28, 1873). And now *Portraits of Places:* "Our observation in a foreign land is extremely superficial, and our remarks are happily not addressed to the inhabitants themselves, who would be sure to exclaim upon the impudence of the fancy-picture" (p. 89; "Italy Revisited," originally published in the *Atlantic Monthly* of April, 1878). Yet, in 1877 James could still experience the Irvingesque pleasure of recognition: the sight of Greenwich Observatory gave him "an amount of pleasure which may at first seem unreasonable. The reason was, simply, that I used to see it as a child, in woodcuts, in school-geographies, and in the corners of large maps. . . . Close at hand was usually something printed about something being at such and such a number of degrees 'east of Greenwich.' Why east of Greenwich? The vague wonder that the childish mind felt on this point gave the place a mysterious importance. . . . Yet there it stood the other day, the precise point from which the great globe is measured" ("London at Midsummer," *Portraits of Places,* p. 242; originally

published in *Lippincott's Magazine* of November, 1877). On the other hand, as early as 1860 in Bonn, in a boyish letter to Perry he could with a self-conscious, perhaps ironic parade of exclamation marks refer to having seen "the most hallowed spots of time-honoured historic Europe" (see Appendix A in Virginia Harlow's *Thomas Sergeant Perry: A Biography* [Durham, N.C., 1950], p. 252).

53. In a letter from Rome to the New York *Tribune,* included in Rahv, *Discovery of Europe,* p. 166.

54. In the preface to Vol. XIV of the New York Edition; see *Art of the Novel,* p. 198.

55. *The American* (1876-77) and *The Portrait of a Lady* (1880-81) can of course both be described as serious problem pieces. But the image of European aristocracy in the former is still close to the conventional stereotypes (see ch. ii above) and the latter deals more with Europeanized Americans than with Europeans (see ch. iii above), whereas the contrasts in the late novels here referred to are between Americans and Europeans.

56. I, 173-74.

57. Whether or not we believe him when he says that he then took in "for all my time, the admirable aspect of the Place and the Colonne Vendôme" (*A Small Boy and Others* [New York, 1913], pp. 53-54).

58. To Perry; see Harlow, p. 252.

59. In the preface to Vol. XIII of the New York Edition; see *Art of the Novel,* p. 195. See the preface to Vol. XIV; *Art of the Novel,* p. 198, for James's discussion of the interest of *"contrasted* things."

60. *Hawthorne,* p. 162.

61. P. 24.

CHAPTER II

1. See the preface to Vol. XIV; *Art of the Novel,* p. 198.

2. See ch. i, p. 28 and n. 52 above.

3. See the preface to Vol. XIII; *Art of the Novel,* pp. 195-96.

4. James's words in the preface to Vol. I; *Art of the Novel,* p. 4.

5. See F. O. Matthiessen, *The James Family* (New York, 1947), p. 254; *The Middle Years* (New York, 1917), pp. 6-7; *Letters,* I, 28, 54.

6. See *Letters,* I, 26-27, 64, 74.

7. *Notebooks,* pp. 23-35, *passim.*

8. *Art of the Novel,* p. 194.

9. In a story entitled "Wigwam versus Almack's" in which an American girl finds herself heir to an English fortune but, after exploring fashionable London life only to be disgusted with its heartlessness, returns to the American West, preferring "the wilderness with one of nature's nobility [here an American Indian] to all the splendors of matrimony in high-life" (*Complete Works* [New York, 1846], p. 294).

10. *Art of the Novel,* p. 22.

11. The phrase "one of nature's noblemen" is James's revision in the New York Edition (p. 91) of the original phrase "a *noble* fellow" (Rinehart Editions, p. 63, James's italics). The original phrase is less close to the traditional American vocabulary for the distinction between natural aristocracy of worth and artificial aristocracy of birth outlined in ch. i above; but the idea, underlined by the italics, is the same. F. O. Matthiessen has suggested that the revisions of *The American* might tell us "how James tried to repair what he had himself come to consider the falsely romantic aspects of his denouement" (*Henry James: The Major Phase*, p. 153). But in the preface, James suggests that he tried to "repair" by heightening certain romantic aspects of the novel rather than by doing away with others. The most obvious improbability, he found, lies in the behavior of the Bellegardes; and the reason for this, he recalled, was that the germ of the novel came to him in the character of Newman. "My concern," he continues, "was to make and to keep Newman consistent; the picture of his consistency was all my undertaking, and the memory of *that* infatuation perfectly abides with me. He was to be the lighted figure. . . . He therefore supremely matters; all the rest matters only as he feels it, treats it, meets it" (*Art of the Novel*, p. 37). Evidently, James heightened the stereotypical, traditional features of Newman. The change of "a *noble* fellow" into "one of nature's noblemen" is part of this. Isadore Traschen's conclusion that James "emphasized and elaborated" on Newman's innocence, that "by heightening Newman's innocence, James later taught him a more affecting lesson in evil, made his loss severer, and his final relinquishment of power morally greater" ("An American in Paris," *American Literature*, XXVI [1954], 77) points to the same thing. For other examples see Note 12 below.

12. I quote here from the original version (Rinehart Editions, pp. 145-46). James's revision for the New York Edition is revealing. Valentin now says: though her "impatiences and appetites" may be average, "she has an exceptional number of ideas." And when Newman doubts whether they are "good" ideas, the Frenchman breaks out: "You people are too wonderful with your goodness. Good for what, please—? They'll be excellent, I warrant, for some things! . . . They'll be good enough to make her, I dare say, one of the celebrities of the future" (pp. 209-10). The effect of this revision is to heighten Valentin's pragmatic distrust of moral absolutes. James added a similar expression, again French, elsewhere in the novel: "Oh, you people, with your moral law—I wonder that with such big words in your mouth you don't all die of choking" (p. 341). Without in any way minimizing what James had come to regard as the romantic features of the novel, such revisions sharpen the international contrast in line with his later distinction between American idealism and European empiricism (see chs. iv through vi above, *passim*). This distinction is part of his later concern with the significance of forms and manners for the scheme of civilization, and related to the distinction between character and culture which he made as early as 1869 (See ch. iii, pp. 79-80, *passim*, above). This complex of ideas, too, is reflected in the revisions; for instance in the change of Newman's "I am a

highly civilized man" (Rinehart Editions, p. 32) to "I have the instincts—have them deeply—if I haven't the forms of a high old civilisation" (New York Edition, p. 45); or in James's introduction of such a phrase as "the discipline of society" (New York Edition, p. 242), which is absent from the original passage.

13. *Art of the Novel*, pp. 26, 34; see also pp. 31-32.

14. "The Story-Teller at Large: Mr. Henry Harland," *Fortnightly Review*, LXIX o.s. (April, 1898), 651.

15. See *Art of the Novel*, pp. 194, 196-97.

16. *Letters*, II, 83.

17. *Hawthorne* (London, 1879), pp. 43-44. The full list occurs almost verbatim in the *Notebooks* (p. 14) as a memorandum for future use in a story, and after his brief return to the United States in 1881 James incorporated something like a travesty of it in "The Point of View" (1882), a mere ingenious pleasantry, as he described it in the prefaces (*Art of the Novel*, p. 213), which contrasts certain typical attitudes toward America. Here, M. Lejaune, of the Académie de France, deplores the absence of art, architecture, and *cocottes*— in fact, of all form, matter, style. And as to literature, just in case we should have missed James's tone, he will admit at most one novelist "with pretensions to literature" who writes about "the adventures of the rich Americans in our corrupt old Europe, where their primeval candour puts the Europeans to shame." To be sure, *"c'est proprement écrit,"* he finally adds, but "terribly pale"—and the last phrase echoes James's reviewers of the time (see R. N. Foley, *Criticism in American Periodicals of the Works of Henry James From 1866 to 1916* [Washington, D.C., 1944], pp. 16-18 and notes).

18. *Letters*, I, 72. For Howells' review see *Atlantic Monthly*, XLV (February, 1880), 282-85, especially pp. 282 and 284.

19. *Notes of a Son and Brother* (New York, 1914), p. 411.

20. Others are discussed briefly in ch. iii above.

21. *William Wetmore Story and His Friends* (Edinburgh and London, 1903), I, 10-11.

22. "I must say I am extremely fond of Paris; you know we Americans always are; we go there when we die.... Of course every one admits that the English hotels are your weak point. There was always the most frightful fog...I know that when you are among yourselves in the country you have the most beautiful time. Of course we have nothing of that sort...some Americans are always apologizing...We have the reputation of always boasting and bragging...The English never apologize...Of course we haven't your country life, and your old ruins, and your great estates, and your leisure class, and all that...I suppose that in England promotion—and all that sort of thing—is fearfully slow...I wish very much my husband were here; but he's dreadfully confined to New York. I suppose you think that is very strange—for a gentleman. But you see we haven't your leisure class." No wonder poor Lord Lambeth listens to her with "a rather ineffectual attention."

23. *Letters*, I, 67-68.

24. See *Art of the Novel,* pp. 206, 280.

25. In the New York Edition the quotation marks are dropped, but they are in *Scribner's* (June, 1899), where the story first came out.

26. "Flickerbridge" is the story of two young Americans, whose engagement breaks up because of the young man's dread of how his fiancée, a journalist, will rant and rave about the "clear still backwater" of Flickerbridge—a dread which turns to veritable horror at the thought that the old lady, its owner, may wake up from the deep doze of her unconsciousness and actually like the chatter. In his preliminary sketch in the *Notebooks* James had thought of her as a cousin of the young man, but by making her represent "the English branch" of the *girl's* family, he added a twist to the old theme of the American claimant, since thus vulgarity, a rash on the shoot of the old tree, appears as the result of trans- plantation to new soil. Such hints are, however, written between the lines. What stands out much more clearly is the contrast between the admiration, vulgar or delicate, of the Americans and the surprised unconsciousness of the old English- woman, who finds the young man's concern for her peace "so very odd."

27. *Notebooks,* p. 291.

28. *Letters,* I, 60. The later passage immediately following is from the preface to Vol. XVIII of the New York Edition; see *Art of the Novel,* p. 280.

29. *Notebooks,* p. 85. For the relevant passages from *Portraits of Places* see ch. i, p. 28 and n. 52 above.

CHAPTER III

1. William Dean Howells, *Heroines of Fiction* (New York and London, 1901), II, 165-66. Among the novels, *The American* and *The Ambassadors* form the only exceptions to this scheme.

2. The passages from the letters James wrote at the time of Minny Temple's death are conveniently assembled in Leon Edel, *Henry James: The Untried Years* (Philadelphia, 1953), pp. 324-31 *passim*; though see also *Letters,* I, 26. Edel makes a detailed and strong case for the great influence James's memory of Minny Temple had on his work. In explaining why Milly Theale of *The Wings of the Dove* had to be American, James says in the preface: "I had from far back mentally projected a certain sort of young American as more the 'heir of all the ages' than any other young person whatever" (*Art of the Novel,* p. 292), and indeed as early as 1884 he made Jackson Lemon in "Lady Bar- barina" apply the same phrase to himself.

3. Dixon Wecter has documented the fact in *The Saga of American Society: A Record of Social Aspirations, 1607-1937* (New York, 1937). Mark Twain's words are to be found in *Mark Twain's Notebook,* ed. Albert Bigelow Paine (New York and London, 1935), p. 336 (see also p. 209), and *Mark Twain in Eruption,* ed. Bernard DeVoto (New York and London, 1940), p. 273. James's remark is in the preface to Vol. XIV of the New York Edition (see *Art of the Novel,* p. 204).

4. Preface to Vol. XIII of the New York Edition; see *Art of the Novel,* pp. 187-93, *passim.* For James's phrases quoted in the next paragraph see *ibid.,* pp. 187-88, and *Letters,* I, 26.

5. P. 167. For another reference to the subject see p. 176.

6. *Heroines of Fiction,* II, 173.

7. *Art of the Novel,* p. 48.

8. *Notebooks,* p. 77. For the words from the preface see *Art of the Novel,* pp. 47-53, *passim.*

9. *Notebooks,* p. 15; italics mine.

10. " 'The Portrait of a Lady' Reprinted," *Scrutiny,* XV (Summer, 1947-48), 237.

11. F. O. Matthiessen has illustrated and analyzed these revisions in *Henry James: The Major Phase,* pp. 152-86. They were not limited to Isabel. In accord with the contrast between America and Europe as more and more in those later years it clarified itself in James's mind, they were designed evidently to heighten the contrast between her uninformed vitality and the formality which in Osmond and, to a lesser extent, in Warburton indicates the atrophy of the spirit.

12. *Image and Idea* (Norfolk, 1949), pp. 53 and 57n. The difference between the European owner and the American collector becomes important in the contrast between Maria Gostrey and Madame de Vionnet of *The Ambassadors;* see ch. iv., p. 103 above.

13. See for instance Randall Stewart, "The Moral Aspects of Henry James's 'International Situation,' " *University Review,* X (1943), 109.

14. P. 351.

15. For the exchange with Wells, which was provoked by a parody of James in Wells's *Boon,* see *Letters,* II, 485-90. For the two passages from the prefaces see *Art of the Novel,* pp. 45, 224. As to "The Figure in the Carpet," James's preface—in particular that part containing his remarks about "operative irony" (*Art of the Novel,* pp. 221-23)—leaves little doubt that the sentence I have quoted, although it describes the convictions of the critics and writers in the story, came from the heart—Percy D. Westbrook's reading of the story as a satire ("The Supersubtle Fry," *Nineteenth-Century Fiction,* VIII [1953], 134-40) notwithstanding.

16. James's phrase in *A Small Boy and Others,* p. 351.

17. Another exception is "Louisa Pallant" (1888), a short story in which "a well-grown, well-washed muscular young American," highly salubrious and suspected of "great innocence"—apparently in James's gallery of Americans the only example of this type—is exposed to the wiles of an American girl whose unmitigated social ambition is the product of a calculated worldly training received at the hands of a worldly mother (the Louisa of the title) during a youth spent largely in European hotels. But since the contrast between the innocence of the young athlete and the corruption of the girl is neither at the center of the story nor related to any international contrast, the story falls really outside the canon of James's international tales.

18. *Letters,* I, 22. What follows completes the contrast: "The pleasantness of the English, on the other side, comes in a great measure from the fact of their each having been dipped into the crucible, which gives them a sort of coating of comely varnish and colour. They have been smoothed and polished by mutual social attrition." Compare this with the description of the Englishman in "The Modern Warning"; see p. 80 above.

19. Ralph Touchett of *The Portrait of a Lady* and Lambert Strether of *The Ambassadors* are two shining exceptions to this rule, but both of them are elegiac figures who, for one reason or another, are able to partake in life as observers only. That they are vibrantly aware of the active fulfilment they have missed is what distinguishes them from their male compatriots.

20. *Notebooks,* p. 82; James's italics.

21. *Ibid.,* p. 82; James's italics again.

22. C. Cestre, "La France dans l'oeuvre de Henry James," *Revue Anglo-Américaine,* X (1932), 114.

23. *Ibid.,* p. 117. Cestre sees the completion of James's "education" in *The Ambassadors,* in Strether's sympathy with "l'épicurisme discret et digne de Chad et de Mme de Vionnet" (*ibid.*)—another example of his blindness to James's bias, which does not allow such a moral identification of Chad and Madame de Vionnet.

CHAPTER IV

1. *Portraits of Places,* pp. 115-18, *passim.*

2. James's words are to be found in the prefaces to Vols. XIV, XVIII, and XXI of the New York Edition; see *Art of the Novel,* pp. 198, 199, 280, 316.

3. Though published after *The Wings of the Dove, The Ambassadors* was written first.

4. See J. W. Beach, *The Method of Henry James* (New Haven, 1918), p. 269.

5. This and the other phrases from James's preface to the novel are to be found in *Art of the Novel,* pp. 308, 310, 316.

6. Again James's preface, *ibid.,* pp. 314, 315.

7. *Ibid.,* pp. 24, 316-17, *passim,* one of the formulations being from the preface to *The American.*

8. *Ibid.,* p. 315.

9. *Ibid.,* p. 189.

10. *Ibid.*

11. Randall Stewart has attributed Chad's anticipated defection to his European "corruption" ("The Moral Aspects of Henry James's 'International Situation,'" *University Review,* X [1943], 109-12), and Yvor Winters, in a generally excellent essay on James, speaks of Chad as the character in this novel "most profoundly affected by the contact with Europe" (*Maule's Curse,* p. 183)— misapprehensions both which seem due, and in Stewart's essay clearly are due,

to the attempt to squeeze James into a pattern whose opposition of "cultural" and "moral" values entirely overlooks his most important contribution to the American analysis of international contrasts.

12. The parallels between Madame de Vionnet and Claire de Cintré of *The American* include further details. Both are the daughters of a French father and an English mother; both have in the marriage of their parents had "no example of comfort"; the fathers of both have died early but left them with "a memory all fondness." Such correspondence of details, some of which are hardly necessary to either story, sets one wondering, inevitably though perhaps vainly, about reasons. What they at any rate underline is the likeness of the two heroines in virtue. As for James's attitude toward adultery, see the passage from the *Notebooks* quoted in chapter vii, p. 147 above. Though belonging to a different context, it may further explain the ease with which Strether accommodates himself to Madame de Vionnet's adultery.

13. The three formulations of William James are to be found in *The Letters of William James,* ed. Henry James (Boston, 1920), I, 147; II, 203-4; and in *The James Family,* ed. F. O. Matthiessen (New York, 1947), p. 313.

14. *Notebooks,* p. 226.

15. The "Project" is printed in the *Notebooks;* see p. 415. To Matthiessen, surprisingly, this last scene serves merely "to exaggerate the negative content of Strether's renunciation." Strether, he argues, "has awakened to a wholly new sense of life. Yet he does nothing at all to fulfill that sense. Therefore, fond as James is of him, we cannot help feeling his relative emptiness." And he sees this as an example of "the contrast in James between imputed and actual values" (*Henry James: The Major Phase,* pp. 38-39, *passim*). The answers to this view come tumbling out of the book thick and fast, and I have given some in the text. But the simplest answer is that Strether's separation from Maria Gostrey involves no renunciation at all on his part since—though for reasons of tact and kindness he cannot tell Maria—he is in love with Madame de Vionnet. And since *she* is in love with Chad, it is hard to see how Strether could have found fulfilment of his love of *her.* Naturally, all this involves resignation on his part, but it is simply the resignation of a man who, at fifty-five, finds that he is too old to catch up on the mistakes of his youth, and who therefore wisely makes the most of that fulness of understanding which is the best "the great cook" has apportioned him.

16. *Notebooks,* pp. 395-96, *passim.*

CHAPTER V

1. Preface to the New York Edition; see *Art of the Novel,* p. 299; James's italics. This chapter owes a large debt to R. P. Blackmur's discussion of *The Wings of the Dove* in an evening seminar which he conducted at Princeton in what must have been the winter of 1950-51. Needless to say, he is not responsible for any errors of mine.

2. *Ibid.*

3. *Ibid.*, p. 288.

4. *Notebooks,* p. 170.

5. *Ibid.,* pp. 171-72.

6. *Art of the Novel,* p. 291.

7. *Ibid.*

8. *Ibid.,* p. 45.

9. *Ibid.,* p. 292.

10. "Mr. Henry James's Later Work," reprinted from the *North American Review* of January, 1903, in *The Question of Henry James,* ed. F. W. Dupee (New York, 1945), p. 7.

11. Strether's phrase is the phrase he uses in his speech in Gloriani's garden (see ch. iv, p. 100 above). But there are other such parallels between the two novels. Milly's sense of communion with the little people in the Regent's Park of London and Strether's in the *Postes et Télégraphes* of Paris both are focal points for important moral statements. And Milly's vision of her "ultimate state" as that of any "poor girl—with her rent to pay" is strikingly close to Strether's view of Marie de Vionnet as "a maidservant crying for her young man" (see ch. iv, p. 104 above).

12. The symbolical unity of the three novels has been emphasized by R. P. Blackmur in his introduction to a reprint of *The Golden Bowl* (New York: Grove Press, 1952), and before this by Quentin Anderson in "Henry James and the New Jerusalem," *Kenyon Review,* VIII (1946), 515-66, and in two essays in *Scrutiny,* XIV (1946-47), 242-51, and XV (1947-48), 12-19. Since this chapter was written, moreover, Anderson has elaborated his views in his *The American Henry James* (New Brunswick, N.J.: Rutgers University Press, 1957). In "The James Brothers," *Sewanee Review,* LVI (1948), 323-28, Henry Bamford Parkes briefly argues that the "main effort of Henry James was to convey, by means of an appropriate aesthetic form, a view of life essentially similar to that which William expressed in [his pragmatic] philosophy" (pp. 326-27). And John Henry Raleigh, in "Henry James: The Poetics of Empiricism," *PMLA,* LXVI (1951), 107-23, relating James's fiction to the ideas of Lockean empiricism, contends that "consciousness, the chief subject matter of [James's] works, was nothing more than an artistic presentation of the idea of the tabula rasa being written upon by experience" (p. 112). Although I have not been concerned with the ideological sources of James's interest in consciousness, my own view of the structural and thematic importance of consciousness in James's late works agrees with the general views of Parkes and Raleigh. Anderson's reading of James's fiction as allegory on the elder James's, the theologian's, "spiritual cosmology" is another matter. To assert, for instance, that *The Ambassadors, The Wings of the Dove,* and *The Golden Bowl* "deal respectively with the three principal churches of our history, the Jewish, the Christian, and the New Church" ("Henry James and the New Jerusalem," p. 554) is, in the absence of external evidence, critical license—at times illuminating license,

since the novelist was a son and in "temperamental sympathy" with the father; but often misleading license, since—as far as we know—he was neither theologian nor disciple in "doctrinal agreement" with the master. Anderson's search leads again and again to findings quite at odds with the novelist's own statements of his intentions. The conclusion of one of his essays is a revealing example: the novelist "knew very well that in our self-righteousness we would love Strether just as he had. But this is more than a literary joke, and it is time we saw the point. Strether is the worst of us all" (*Scrutiny,* XV [1947], 19). This may be what the theologian would have said of Strether, but it is not what the novelist did say. It is not exegesis, not explication of the author's intent, but moral criticism of the author.

CHAPTER VI

1. Preface to Vol. XIII of the New York Edition; see *Art of the Novel,* p. 189. The phrase "sublime consensus" is to be found in the preface to Vol. XIV; see *ibid.,* p. 203.

2. *Ibid.,* pp. 329-30.

3. Preface to Vol. XIV of the New York Edition, *ibid.,* p. 199.

4. F. O. Matthiessen, *Henry James: The Major Phase* (New York, 1944), p. 102.

5. *Ibid.,* p. 101.

6. James "seems to take Mr. Verver at his own estimate"; he "never probes the implications" of the anomalous fact that Mr. Verver "applies 'the same measure of value to such different pieces of property as old Persian carpets... and new human acquisitions' "—thus Matthiessen (*op. cit.,* pp. 89, 100). F. W. Dupee sees Maggie and her father as "doubtless" exemplifying James's "ideal program for the class" to which they belong (*Henry James* [New York, 1951], p. 261). Similarly Elizabeth Stevenson, who believes that James meant Adam Verver to represent "the rich man converted," the rich man "who has set aside money-making" for "what James called life" (*The Crooked Corridor* [New York, 1949], p. 32).

7. James's phrase in *Notebooks,* p. 131.

8. Ferner Nuhn, *The Wind Blew from the East* (New York, 1942), pp. 135, 149.

9. *The Destructive Element* (London, 1935), p. 91.

10. Nuhn, *op. cit.,* p. 149.

11. *Notebooks,* p. 131.

12. P. 55.

13. Preface to Vol. XIV of the New York Edition; see *Art of the Novel,* p. 203.

14. Stephen Spender has said that in James a failure of "intelligence in life" may "amount to a moral failing" but that "it does not follow that intelligence alone is morality," since in *The Golden Bowl* "it is Maggie's love that

saves the marriages" (*The Destructive Element*, p. 92). This may seem true until one finds, as the later James tempts one to find, that love and sympathy as well as *real* tact are in his world possible only to the high intelligence. For like Iago's vaunted subtlety, Kate Croy's and Charlotte Stant's intelligence—the former's "talent for life," the latter's "too perfect competence"—suffer a kind of defeat because they come in conflict with something beyond their reach. Near the end Amerigo calls Charlotte "stupid," and although this does not define James's sense of her, Charlotte's judgment in fact does fail again and again. There is in particular an early conversation between her and Amerigo in which her condescending pity for Maggie's modesty and goodness—reminiscent of Kate Croy's attitude toward Milly Theale—is both dishonest and obtuse, so that it combines the immoral and the unintelligent. Amerigo is aware of this; the scene is one of many subtle dramatizations of the difference between them. Fanny Assingham makes similar though less interested mistakes. Indeed, the comic conversations between her and her husband function largely as a kind of inverted chorus, contributing elucidation not so much by just comment as by pointed misinterpretation. Matthiessen has pointed out that, while Fanny Assingham with her passion for "scrutinizing the motives of her friends" may seem typical of what to many readers "is worst in James," she is treated ironically; that James intended her *soi-disant* lucidity to reveal itself as "barren." But whether this means that "in James' scale of values there is a higher morality than that of 'high Intelligence'" (*Henry James: The Major Phase*, pp. 94-95) is at least debatable. The irony of Fanny's question, "what is morality but high intelligence," may lie in her notion of intelligence as well as of morality. The impact, certainly, of her repeated mistakes in judgment is not so much that her morality is at fault as that she inveterately overrates her own perspicacity. Her pronouncement that "the forms are two thirds of conduct" is an example of this primarily because it is made in connection with Charlotte's observation of the "forms." For it is an important part of the significance of the contrast between Charlotte and Amerigo, the Europeanized American and the European, that there are forms and forms and that some forms alone are nothing. That Charlotte should trust to what she calls "the commonest tact" as a refuge in their predicament surprises Amerigo—"as if," he feels, "this principle alone would suffice to light their way." And again one is reminded of *The Wings of the Dove,* this time of Densher's doomed attempt to rely on "tact" for finding his way through the maze of his moral predicament. Amerigo, polished as he is, more polished than anyone, perceives how external, how much a mere convenience, Charlotte's tact is. His own is a matter of the heart as much as of training; it is part of the natural grace, the "handsomeness and friendliness" which, as James wrote in a letter of 1886, could make even "vulgarity" strike him in Italy as "the exaggeration of a merit and not, as in England and the U.S., of a defect" (*Letters,* I, 122). The figure of Amerigo is an expression of James's lifelong sympathy with the Latin civilization, in contrast with which England and America were to him much alike. And this explains why Densher's moral predicament is much more tortuous than Amerigo's; why his fall, though in a way it is a Fortunate Fall, leaves him with a sense of odium of which Amerigo is quite incapable. The distinction between Amerigo and Charlotte, too, is related to this, since *her* tact, a matter of convenient propriety, of skilful management and calculated address, is a necessity of her dimmed sense of wrong, while his is simple consideration, sympathetic perception of the needs and rights of others without conscious moral flavor. Perhaps the question whether in James's world morality is in the final analysis "intelligence" depends on one's understanding of the terms. The more one reads James, at any rate, the more one becomes aware of the close connection between his basic ethical values—sympathy, decency, candor—and the lucid consciousness which is so fundamental a virtue or so desirable a goal of his heroes and heroines that it determined more and more the very structure of his fiction.

CHAPTER VII

1. See Philip Rahv's interesting discussion of such treatments of James in "Attitudes Toward Henry James," first published in the *New Republic,* February 15, 1943. This essay is reprinted in *The Question of Henry James,* ed. F. W. Dupee.

2. "Paris, London, Rome ... have heightened his power of refraction; but his lenses themselves remain more trans-Atlantic than many of his readers are apt to suppose.... in the employment of his method upon English themes Mr. James has exposed an essentially un-English mind.... If Maggie Verver is not to be seen as American, some of us will not be able to see her at all" (M. Sturge Gretton, "Mr. Henry James and His Prefaces," *Contemporary Review,* CI [January, 1912], 70, 72). Marie-Anne de Bovet, "Un écrivain cosmopolite, Henry James," *La Nouvelle Revue* (1891), p. 535, quoted in Cyrille Arnavon, *Les Lettres américaines devant la critique française (1887-1917)* (Paris, 1951), p. 88. Eliot's remark occurs in an essay "On Henry James," first published in the *Little Review* of August, 1918, and reprinted in *The Question of Henry James,* ed. F. W. Dupee, p. 108.

3. "Americans Abroad," the *Nation,* XXVII (October 3, 1878), 208-9. It is of course curious that strangers should need to be told that they are outsiders, but that the warning was necessary only shows once more how much Americans were still inclined to regard Europe as their "old home."

4. *Letters,* I, 55.

5. *Portraits of Places* (New York, 1948), p. 115.

6. To Hamlin Garland, who visited him in Rye in 1906, James said, "If I were to live my life again I would be American—steep myself in it—know no other. I would study its beautiful side. This mixture of Europe and America is disastrous. It makes man neither one thing nor the other" (Hamlin Garland, "London Notes, 1906," quoted in B. R. McElderry, "Hamlin Garland and Henry James," *American Literature,* XXIII [1952], 442). As "a final ironic com-

ment on the relationship of these two oddly assorted American realists,"
McElderry points out that "as Garland grew older his sympathy with James's
expatriation increased" (*ibid.,* p. 445). In 1913 James warned Amy Lowell
against making his "mistake": "I have cut myself off from America, where
I belonged," she reports him as saying (see S. Foster Damon, *Amy Lowell*
[Boston, 1935], p. 212). In the letter which was read at Howells' seventy-fifth
birthday dinner in 1912, James wrote: "I seem to myself to have faltered and
languished, to have missed more occasions than I have grasped, while you have
piled up your monument just by remaining at your post. For you have had the
advantage, after all, of breathing an air that has suited and nourished you;
of sitting up to your neck, as I may say—or at least up to your waist—amid the
sources of your inspiration" (*Letters,* II, 223).

7. *Letters,* II, 492; James's italics.

8. *Letters,* II, 477-78.

9. For instance by Edna Kenton in an essay in the James Number of
Hound & Horn (1934), reprinted in 1945 in *The Question of Henry James,*
ed. F. W. Dupee. Miss Kenton's emphasis on the purely external aspect of the
situation is probably due to the general purpose of her essay, which is to correct
the notorious misconceptions about James's "expatriatism." But such emphasis
obscures the issue. For in arguing that the term *expatriate* "covers James's situation during the last few months of his life" (*The Question of Henry James,*
p. 132) only, she assumes a sense of the term so purely formal or political as
to place it quite outside her own arguments. The real issue, and the issue with
which her essay on the whole so effectively deals, is not the simple abrogation of
citizenship itself but the emotional and intellectual attitudes behind it.

10. *Letters,* II, 491.

11. *Letters,* II, 479.

12. For the letters to William James and Edith Wharton see *Letters,* I,
141-43; II, 57; for the confession of his social ordeal, *Letters,* I, 69. For Edith
Wharton's recollections see *A Backward Glance* (New York and London, 1934),
pp. 173-74, *passim.*

13. In working out the details of "A London Life," James records in June,
1887, that he must modify the germ of the story because he cannot "depict in
an American magazine, a woman carrying on adulteries under her daughter's
eyes. That case," he imagines, "is in America so rare as to be almost abnormal"
(*Notebooks,* p. 77). In March, 1888, a somewhat similar change in the development of another story has become advisable "because of the prejudices," not of
the American, but now of the "Anglo-Saxon reader" (*ibid.,* p. 88). Not only
the change from *American* to *Anglo-Saxon* but also the word *prejudices* is here
significant, suggesting as it does his sense of the relativity of sexual morals. In
April, 1894, he worried again about the difficulty of presenting "the 'sexual'
side" of still another theme, now "to English readers" (*ibid.,* p. 157)—with
which the blurring of *American* and *English* is complete. On vacation in Paris,
James might—as Edith Wharton remembered and as some of the essays in

Portraits of Places show—enjoy observing the differences "in the mental attitude and the moral conventions" (*A Backward Glance,* p. 307); but in writing for an English-speaking public he felt that they created problems—unless indeed one might build a story on these very differences, as he did in *The Ambassadors.* For the other citations in this paragraph see *Notebooks,* pp. 170, 174, 188 (James's italics), 226.

14. Among his major novels, only *The Wings of the Dove* deals with contrasts within the Anglo-Saxon world. Nevertheless, the idea of "human Anglo-Saxonism" remained active in his mind. In revising "Daisy Miller" for the New York Edition, for instance, he could let his Anglo-Saxon consciousness steal into a story which originally had nothing to do with it: he could let Winterbourne reflect "on that depth of Italian subtlety, *so strangely opposed to Anglo-Saxon simplicity,* which . . ." (New York Edition, XVIII, 58; the phrase here italicized does not appear in the original version).

15. James's most extended discussion of the international theme is to be found in the prefaces to Vols. XIII, XIV, and XVIII of the New York Edition. For the citations in this paragraph see *Art of the Novel,* pp. 153, 198-203, *passim.*

16. To be sure, moral considerations are rarely absent from his fiction. But while in his early international stories the manners of a people may serve as a measure of its moral level, in his later they do not. While in *The American,* for instance, inferior manners illustrate inferior morals, in *The Ambassadors* the conflict between the different sets of manners is a means for dramatizing different sources of moral feeling. And the same is true of *The Wings of the Dove* and *The Golden Bowl.*

17. *Letters,* I, 418. The citation immediately following is from the preface to Vol. XV of the New York Edition; see *Art of the Novel,* p. 223.

18. Virginia Harlow, *Thomas Sergeant Perry: A Biography, and Letters to Perry from William, Henry, and Garth Wilkinson James* (Durham, N. C., 1950), pp. 284-85.

19. F. O. Matthiessen, *The James Family,* p. 303. T. S. Eliot's phrase is to be found in the previously cited essay; see *The Question of Henry James,* ed. Dupee, p. 110.

CHAPTER VIII

1. *Literature and Life* (New York and London, 1902), p. 205, and *Heroines of Fiction* (New York and London, 1901), II, 165.

2. "Occasional Paris," in *Portraits of Places* (New York, 1948), p. 115. (The essay was first published under the title of "Paris Revisited" in *The Galaxy,* January, 1878.) In 1884, James sounded the same note in an essay on Turgenieff, another expatriate; and considering how many of his comments on the Russian apply to himself, it is difficult not to see in them reflections of how he felt about his own state. "Cosmopolite that he had become by the force of circum-

stances, his roots had never been loosened in his native soil" (*Partial Portraits* [London, 1894], p. 292). This is James's second essay on Turgenieff, written shortly after the Russian's death and first published in the *Atlantic Monthly* in January, 1884. James's first essay on the Russian appeared first in the *North American Review* in April, 1874, and was later included in *French Poets and Novelists* (London, 1878). It is striking how much of James's description of Turgenieff in 1874 fits what he himself was or aspired to be: "He belongs to the limited class of very careful writers." "His line is narrow observation." He is "a storyteller who has taken notes." His "object is constantly the same,—that of finding an incident, a person, a situation, *morally* interesting." "Deep into the mind he is always attempting to look." And "always with our author, the drama is quite uncommented; the poet never plays chorus; situations speak for themselves." Turgenieff's young Russian girls even "have to our sense a touch of the faintly acrid perfume of the New England temperament ... strength of will—the power to resist, to wait, to attain." If about Turgenieff's expatriation this early essay says little, one suspects it is because at the time of writing it James himself had not yet settled abroad and expatriation was no immediate problem of his own. To be sure, he remarks that Turgenieff was "a cosmopolitan, a dweller in many cities, and a frequenter of many societies," and he explains his "manner" as residing in the "union of an aristocratic temperament with a democratic intellect." In the second essay ten years later he calls this earlier remark *inane.* Now he emphasizes that Turgenieff "felt and understood the opposite sides of life" (p. 296), and it is evident that expatriation has meantime become a fact the writer himself has had to face.

3. *Art of the Novel,* pp. 198, 280.

4. Pp. 23-24. (He was actually thirty-eight years old.)

5. Logan Pearsall Smith reports that in 1895 James told him with unmistakable feeling that if he really intended to dedicate his life to writing, *Loneliness* was the word which above all others he had to "inscribe upon" his "banner" (*Unforgotten Years* [Boston, 1939], pp. 219-20).

6. *Letters,* I, 419, 420; II, 23, 25, 31, 32. In addition to a lecture tour, he was thinking also of a collected edition to be brought out in America. After his return to Rye, he went to work on the laborious task of revising his works and of writing the prefaces to the New York Edition, which began to come out in 1907, the year in which he also published *The American Scene.* In 1910, he returned to America once more, this time to accompany William, who had fallen seriously ill in Europe. Shortly after they arrived, William sank rapidly and died; and as a kind of commemoration of their lifelong friendship, Henry, at the suggestion of William's wife, wrote the two autobiographical volumes *A Small Boy and Others* (1913) and *Notes of a Son and Brother* (1914). All this explains why in the eleven years left him after his return from the climactic trip of 1904-5 he produced so little fiction compared with his earlier output. Twice, moreover, he was ill for prolonged periods, and the outbreak of war in 1914 brought his

artistic life almost to a standstill. Except for *The Outcry* (1911), the result of his renewed theatrical ambitions, written as a play but for publication hastily and cursorily transformed into a "novel," *The Golden Bowl* is the last novel he completed. In addition to the items cited, he published a number of short stories, and at his death left behind two novel fragments, *The Sense of the Past* and *The Ivory Tower*, and the beginning of *The Middle Years*, a third autobiographical volume—all published posthumously.

7. *Letters*, II, 48-49. For William's alarm see *The Letters of William James* (Boston, 1920), II, 189.

8. *Letters*, II, 28, 30.

9. *Letters*, II, 31.

10. See *Notebooks*, pp. 151, 281; *American Scene*, p. 25. Monteith has been cheated by a friend charged with the care of his American property; this is the secret of his grief. James used this motif of the unfaithful steward several times in his late American stories—not only in "A Round of Visits," but also in "Crapy Cornelia," where it is merely alluded to, and in *The Ivory Tower*, where it is central. Even much earlier, however, the same motif occurs in "The Impressions of a Cousin" (1883), a story which grew out of "a matter in the history of Mme de Sévigné" (*Notebooks*, p. 19) but which James conceived and laid in America, during his visit of 1881. Indeed, greed is of course a constant motif in James's fiction (see Bradford A. Booth, "Henry James and the Economic Motif," *Nineteenth-Century Fiction*, VIII [September, 1953], 141-50), and what characterizes American life in these late stories is not greed but the lack of "manners" which accompanies it, the *rankness* of the money passion or, in the words of *The Ivory Tower*, of the "awful game of grab."

11. *The Question of Our Speech. The Lesson of Balzac: Two Lectures* (Boston and New York, 1905), pp. 14, 47.

12. James's words in a review of Howells' *A Foregone Conclusion*, in *Nation*, XX (January 7, 1875), 12. The confession cited later in the same paragraph comes from the preface to Vol. XVIII of the New York Edition; see *Art of the Novel*, p. 270. The whole passage about "those aweful young women" is worth reading in full. For the essay on "The Manners of American Women" see *Harper's Bazar*, XLI (April, May, June, July, 1907), *passim*, but especially pp. 648-51.

13. *The American Scene*, ed. W. H. Auden (New York, 1946), p. 431.

14. *Notebooks*, p. 129; *The Question of Our Speech*, p. 39; *Harper's Bazar*, XLI (June, 1907), 537.

15. *A Small Boy and Others*, pp. 214-16, *passim*.

16. See ch. v, n. 12, above.

17. William James's phrase is to be found in a letter quoted in F. O. Matthiessen, *The James Family*, p. 313. Henry's famous dictum about the "thinly-composed" society of New England occurs in his *Hawthorne* (London, 1879), p. 45, but in *The American Scene* (p. 321) he still contrasts the "thinness" of

American life with the "superimposed densities," the "thousand thicknesses of tradition," which are part of life in Europe. For the "great modern collapse" see *Notebooks,* p. 196; for Edith Wharton her *A Backward Glance* (New York and London, 1934), p. 175; for James's confession *Letters,* II, 297-98.

18. Harlow, *Thomas Sergeant Perry,* p. 258.

19. *Essays in London and Elsewhere* (New York, 1893), p. 150.

20. As far as James's notes permit us to guess, the other novel which he left unfinished, *The Sense of the Past* (1917), was to treat the problem of the American relation to Europe once more in terms of a contrast between two American attitudes toward that relation: between the hero's desire for a place "where things have happened" and where "the continuity of life" has inscribed itself on surfaces and objects, and on the other hand, the heroine's election of America, the place which, as she puts it, "denies the old at every turn and contains so few objects and surfaces." Aurora Coyne—and it is difficult not to see intention in a name which almost asks to be translated, "the rising light of the market place"—feels that it is time for Americans to abandon their great "fool's errand" across the sea and instead "to try and make something" at home. To Ralph Pendrel this is simply "the new cry," all the more new for now being heard among the "upper classes." Ralph and Aurora are latter-day variants of the passionate pilgrim and the social critic of an earlier day; and their story was to dramatize, apparently, a reconciliation of the two familiar American attitudes toward Europe—a purpose which receives emphasis from the fact that James employs a modification of the old theme of the American claimant. In England, exchanging his identity with an ancestor of a century or so earlier, Ralph Pendrel literally steps into the past, getting thus "the thing he has always wanted to have still more than historic records can give it" (*Notebooks,* p. 363). What this miraculous escapade does for him, however, is to make him feel a malaise increasingly terrifying, so that his final return to the present is pure relief (see *ibid.,* p. 367). The "Notes" to the novel printed in the New York Edition end with the allusion to a final scene which "prefigures Ralph's reunion, not to say union" with Aurora. But while his preparation for this symbolic conclusion is not hard to see, hers is left vague, and vague therefore too the fusion of their originally conflicting points of view. If in this *tour de force* the excursion into the past is for the American inevitably an excursion into the English past, this is due once more to James's sense of the close Anglo-Saxon affinities between America and England, of "shared instincts and ideals, of a communion of race and tongue, temper and tradition," as he put it in a war essay written about the same time (*Within the Rim and Other Essays, 1914-1915* [London, 1918], p. 35). The contrast between the civilization from which Ralph comes and the more brutal one into which he penetrates is at any rate more a contrast between present and past than between America and Europe.

21. *Letters,* II, 384.

Index

193